WELSH MILITIA AND VOLUNTEER CORPS
1757-1908

WELSH MILITIA AND VOLUNTEER CORPS
1757-1908

1 : ANGLESEY & CAERNARFONSHIRE

By Bryn Owen

Palace Books

First impression: February 1989

Hardback ISBN 1 871904 00 5

Cover design by Jac Jones
Typesetting by Stiwdio Mei
Printing by W.O. Jones

Published by
PALACE BOOKS
Caernarfon · Gwynedd · Wales

PROFILE OF THE AUTHOR

Bryn Owen was educated at Dolgellau Grammar School for Boys, Merionethshire, in which County he was born in 1928.

On leaving School, he enlisted in the Royal Navy on a regular engagement, and was in due course promoted from the Lower Deck and commissioned as a Gunnery Officer.

In 1975, after his retirement from the service, he became involved with The Welch Regiment Museum, and in 1978 was appointed its Curator.

Bryn, a regular contributor to military and other journals, lives with his Wife and Son at Radyr, Cardiff, where most of his spare time is devoted to research and writing. He is a Fellow of the Museums Association and an adviser on military matters to the Council of Museums in Wales.

Previously published work

Glamorgan — Its Gentlemen and Yeomanry. Starling Press, 1983.

FOREWORD BY
MAJOR GENERAL R.M. LLEWELLYN OBE
GENERAL OFFICER COMMANDING WALES

The need for effective volunteer forces to play their part in providing for the defence of the realm is as crucial now as it has ever been. Today's Territorial Army is held in high esteem being an integral part of the Army's "order of battle." However, while the Regular Army's regimental history, together with that of current Territorial Battalions and Regiments, is kept very much alive, it is easy to forget that many fine Militia and Volunteer Regiments, whose badges and insignia are no longer worn on parade, have a noble past and played an important part in our nation's history and heritage. To the general public they are virtually unknown. My forbears served in many such regiments from North, South and West Wales and I have often been embarrassed by my ignorance of the origins, functions and structure of the Militia and other Auxiliary Forces of the Crown. Bryn Owen's series of histories covering, in due course, every county in Wales, is greatly to be welcomed. Not only is it badly needed to fill gaps in our knowledge and in our records, but he imparts to his task, a great deal of scholarship and a flair for making history come alive.

I am privileged to have been asked to write this foreword to the first volume covering the counties of Anglesey and Caernarfon. After thirty years service in the Royal Welch Fusiliers it has been fascinating to trace the many links with that Regiment. As a Welshman it has given me a new insight into the extent of the contribution made by the Welsh Militia and Volunteers Corps to our national heritage. Above all it is an eminently readable and enjoyable book which will rouse the interest of the ordinary reader as well as the scholar and the specialist. I much look forward to further volumes in the series.

Brecon 1989

AUTHOR'S NOTE

This book does not pretend to be a comprehensive history of the services of the Militia and Volunteers of Anglesey and Caernarfonshire, but could perhaps be described as an abridged version of same were such to exist. It is more an attempt to bring under one cover basic and other interesting information relating to the contribution made by the Civilian Soldiers of both Counties to national defence over a period of some one and a half centuries of Great Britain's history, and clarify the role and terms of service of the various non-regular armed bodies which were active between 1757 and 1908.

The information offered is directed not only towards those who are keen on military matters, but also at the increasing numbers who today delve deeply into local and personal family history, particularly those who like myself have roots in that part of Wales now called Gwynedd.

Such persons, if not already aware of the fact will discover the close links which exist between the military and social history of the counties under discussion, as the demands made by the one had much effect on the shaping and direction of the other. Making use of the foundations provided, it is hoped that the local historian will be encouraged to further expand the theme by making use of the documents, newspapers and other material which is to this day preserved in that excellent and well run establishment, the Gwynedd Area Records Office, and as a result draw more attention to the importance of preserving for the benefit of future generations, the few Colours and other historical relics, which together with the published work, link us quite firmly to a military heritage which is second to none.

I pay tribute on this page to the late Hugh J. Owen, one time Clerk of the Peace and of the County Council of the County of Merioneth, whose work on a similar subject for that County encouraged me to try to follow suit many years ago.

I dedicate the book to those men and women of Anglesey and Caernarfonshire who during the two Great Wars of the present century, gave unstinting and loyal service to our Country in the Armed Forces of the Crown.

Bryn Owen,
Radyr, Cardiff,
1st August, 1988.

ACKNOWLEDGEMENTS

Cardiff Central Library
Chester Central Library
Clwyd Area Records Office, Hawarden and Ruthin
Christie's of Kensington
Gloucester Central Library
Gwynedd Area Records Office, Caernarfon and Llangefni
Hereford Central Library
Ministry of Defence Central Library
Museum of Welsh Antiquities, Bangor
National Army Museum
National Library of Wales, Aberystwyth
Public Records Office, Kew.
Royal Institution of South Wales, Swansea
Royal Welch Fusiliers Museum, Caernarfon Castle

Aubrey Bowden
W.Y. Carman and Lord Danvers Osborn
D.G. Glover
P. Haythornthwaite
Norman Holme
John Carey Hughes
Bernadette Hunter
Ivor Wynne Jones
Hugh King
Clive Lewis
Norman Litchfield
Geoffrey Archer Parfitt
Richard Scollins
John Tyler
Ray Westlake
G. Haulfryn Williams
and to those other individuals, too numerous to mention, who over the years assisted in the compiling of this record.

CONTENTS

THE MILITIA

In England, the origins of Militia can be traced back to the Fyrd of Saxon times — a force, whose members, in addition to their civil occupations, trained in the use of weapons for the purpose of both local and national defence. The Fyrd over years developed into the General Levy, which like its predecessor was based on the obligation of able bodied men to render service within the boundaries of their own districts, and in the event of invasion or rebellion, march to any part of the country to serve as directed.

In Wales, the principles of this system were imposed upon the population gradually, and was part of a long period of pacification.

During the reign of Edward VI, influential persons were appointed in each district to 'array' and lead the Levy. These Commissioners of Array were the forerunners, in respect of Militia, of the Lords Lieutenant, who up until the late 19th Century controlled and administered the Force in each County.

Possibly the earliest record relating to the activities of a form of Militia in the Counties of Anglesey and Caernarfonshire is that Return of Manpower known as The Great Muster which was initiated by Act 30, Henry VIII of 1539. It records for Anglesey, 1,228 men, of whom 620 were harnessed, and for Caernarfonshire, 2,429 men of which 729 were harnessed — that is to say, properly equipped for War[1]. For later years, references to the contribution made by both Counties can be found in the Calendar of the Council in the Marches for Wales, the Wynn of Gwydir Papers in the National Library, Aberystwyth, and in locally preserved documents relating to the activities of the landed gentry.

The term 'Trained' or 'Train' Bands was used to describe such bodies of men in the 17th Century, but by the reign of Charles 1 they were also referred to as Militia. It will be remembered that a dispute as to whether the King or Parliament should control Militia was one of the factors which led to bloody Civil War and the execution of a King. The restoration of his son to the throne in 1660 saw a country which was sick of military rule allow the foundations to be laid for only a small Standing Army and place the counterbalancing Militia firmly in the hands of the nation's landed gentry.

In 1684, the Duke of Beaufort in his capacity as Lord President of the Council of Wales made a tour of the Principality for the purpose of making a "General visitation of his commands there". Thomas Dinely, a member of his entourage, recorded his progress, and gave an account of the Militia Regiments, then a mixture of both Horse and Foot, which the Duke inspected.

"The Militia of Caernarvonshire consisteth of three companies of foot and troop of horse." During the inspection "laudable exercise and fireings were performed, having been called to it by beat of drum at, and before the break of day." That event took place in Conway after which the party moved across the country towards Anglesey.

There, the Duke was greeted by the Militia of that county "with volleyes of shot at his putting foot on this Island." The Anglesey Militia is described as consisting of one Troop of Horse and four Companies of Foot, the former carrying a Standard of crimson flowered damask with gold silk fringe and tassells. The Foot Companies carried blue Colours with the exception of the Beaumaris Company whose Colour was red[2].

In 1757 a Militia Act[3] changed entirely the method of raising men for the force and the liablility to provide them became the responsibility of the Counties and their Parishes as opposed to hitherto appointed individuals. The chief powers nonetheless remained firmly in the hands of the Lords Lieutenant with the Militia still being regarded as a counterbalance to the Standing Army and controlled by Parliament rather than by the Crown. The Act confined Militia to the Infantry role and did much to improve its organisation and quality, but sadly, a 'Substitute System'[4] destroyed any chance of it being representative of universal national service, and instead allowed the more affluent members of the community to shirk their duty and throw the responsibility for their protection and that of the nation generally on to the shoulders of that section of the population which had not the means to purchase exemption.

The Militia was embodied for Garrison duty at home during the Seven Years War, The War of the American Revolution and the French Revolutionary War, but undoubtedly the most important and interesting period in the history of the force and its individual regiments is the period 1803-1816 when in addition to essential Garrison duties at home, the Militia provided an essential and most valuable reserve of trained manpower for the Regular Army. Thousands of Militiamen volunteered for service with the Regiments of the Line, and it is true to say that Wellington's campaign in the Iberian Peninsula would at times have been difficult, if not impossible, to pursue successfully were it not for the reinforcements which were made available for his Army from the various Militia Regiments at home. Both Anglesey and Caernarfonshire Regiments put up their fair quota of men, and were represented in most of the great land battles of that period.

"A successful War seems to demoralise a national military spirit, and military inactivity is usually the sequence" — so stated B.E. Sargeaunt in his History of the Monmouthshire Militia[5], and such was the situation for many years following the final defeat of Napoleon at Waterloo. The Militia slid slowly into obscurity, with the laws which ordered its annual training rescinded and the Ballot which maintained it at strength suspended. Such matters were after 1816 submitted annually to Parliament for decision which resulted in some sporadic Militia training between 1818 and 1825, and then not until 1831, when a state of civil unrest demanded a short resuscitation. For the next twenty years or so all that remained to remind the nation of the existence of the force was the presence in each county town of a small Permanent Staff who paraded for Church on Sundays. Officers continued to be appointed but, with Weapons returned to Ordnance and with no men to train, the Militia was reduced to nothing more than a force on paper.

The succession of Louis Napoleon to the Presidency of France, French military posturing and fears concerning Russian ambitions in the Middle East led Government c.1850 to some serious reappraisal of matters relating to home defence. One outcome was the Militia Act of 1852 which directed that the Militia, hitherto a force raised by compulsory ballot, be in the future raised entirely by voluntary enlistment. The Militia Ballot remained suspended, but with the proviso that it could be reintroduced if voluntary enlistment failed to produce the numbers required. Some 80,000 men were to be raised for the force by 1853, recruits enlisting for five years during which period they would in the first instance produce themselves for 21 days training annually. The years of decline for Militia ended, as in every county the Lieutenancy made arrangements for recruiting the numbers required and for the reintroduction of annual training. From that date through to April 1908 the Militia trained annually, and some regiments were embodied for Garrison duty during the periods of the Crimean War and the Indian Mutiny.

In 1871 there commenced a long series of Army reforms, the most immediate of which was directed at the Militia. An Act[7] transferred all power and control of the Force from the Lords Lieutenant to the Crown, the force thereafter being paid and clothed according to Regulations fixed by Royal Warrant in the same way as the Regular Army. The culmination of the same series of reforms took place in 1881 when the Militia, and the Infantry in particular were drawn closer under the wing of the Regular Army, the latter becoming numbered Battalions of the recently established Territorial Line Infantry Regiments.

During the South African (Boer) War of 1899-1902, most Militia Regiments were embodied for short periods of Garrison Duty, whilst others proceeded on active service with the Regular Army at the seat of War. Their service at the front, albeit mainly on the lines of communication, was vital to the success of the campaign.

The story of the Militia serving under that ancient title ends in 1908, when reorganisation of the Land Forces of the Crown saw the Militia cease to be raised in the United Kingdom. The implimentation of the Territorial and Reserve Forces Act of 1907[8] at that date resulted in the disbandment of many of the old Militia regiments, and the conversion of what remained into units of the Army Special Reserve.

The term 'Militia' in its loosest form was used to describe the Supplementary Reserve until 1953. The last of the old Force had by that date slipped quietly away into obscurity, a sad and unpublicised demise, as the old Constitutional Force was in more ways than one the tap root of our present day home defence system.

Footnotes.

1. The Constitutional Force. Colonel Jackson Hay, CB, CMG.
2. The Account of the Progress of His Grace, Henry, 1st Duke of Beaufort, Lord President of the Council in Wales and Warden of the Marches, through Wales in 1684. Thomas Dineley.
3. Act 30. Geo 11, c.25
4. A system whereby a person selected by Ballot to serve in the Militia, and who did not wish to render personal service, was allowed to provide at his own expense a Sustitute i.e., a man willing to serve on his behalf. Alternatively, such men could pay a Fine to the Lieutenancy, which money, in full or in part, was used to provide a Cash Bounty to draw in a Substitute to make up the required quota.
5. The Royal Monmouthshire Militia. B.E. Sargeaunt, RUSI, London, 1910.
6. Act 15 & 16 Victoria, c.50
7. Act 34 & 35 Victoria, c.86. s.6.
8. Act Edward VII, c.9. 2nd August, 1907.

THE MILITIA
1762-1908

THE ANGLESEY MILITIA

1762 Anglesey Militia
1792 Royal Anglesey Fusiliers
1810 Royal Anglesey Light Infantry
1852 Royal Anglesey Rifle Corps
1852 Royal Anglesey Light Infantry
1860 Royal Caernarvon and Anglesey Rifles
1867 Royal Anglesey Light Infantry
1877 Royal Anglesey Engineers Militia
1908 Royal Anglesey Royal Engineers (Special Reserve)

Commanding Officers

1778 Herbert Jones of Llynon
1780 William Peacoke
1782 Herbert Jones of Llynon
1793 William Evans of Glanalaw
1795 Hon Arthur Paget
1803 William Lewis Hughes of Lleiniog
1853 Thomas Peers Williams of Craig y Don
1881 T.L. Hampton Lewis of Henllys
1900 Sir R.H. Williams Bulkeley, Bt.

Precedence Numbers

1780 — 4. 1803 — 69. 1833 — 61.

A VIEW OF THE IMPORTANT MILITARY CAMP AT COXHEATH, KENT, IN 1779, AT WHICH PLACE BOTH THE ANGLESEY AND CAERNARFONSHIRE REGIMENTS OF MILITIA WERE PRESENT.

By kind permission of The Welch Regiment Museum, Cardiff.

1762-1777

The passing of the Militia Act of 1757 did not result in the immediate raising of a regiment of Infantry Militia in the county, and it would appear that the Lord Lieutenant found it no easy matter to comply with its demands. In a reply dated 7th June, 1759, to an enquiry regarding progress which he had received from the Secretary of State for War, Earl Cholmondeley had this to say: "In obedience to His Majesty's command, I take the liberty to acquaint you that notwithstanding my repeated Letters and Advertisments in the *Gazette* for the meeting of the Gentlemen of the County of Anglesey to form a Corps of Officers for the Militia, not one gentleman's name has been returned to me as willing to serve."[1]

It was not until 1762 that the efforts met with some success. In that year, the regiment required by the Act was finally raised, and the men, the majority of whom had been selected by ballot, assembled for training. They were issued with Arms on the 19th November, and on completion of a short training period dismissed to their homes.

In terms of stength, the regiment resembled only a Company, as the quota of Militiamen demanded from the county was 80, a figure which remained unchanged until 1796. It must be presumed that between 1762 and 1778, the regiment assembled annually for training, and was kept up to strength by enforcement of the ballot when replacements became necessary.

1778—1782

In 1778, France declared War on Great Britain in support of the American Colonists and assembled in Brittany an Army ready for an invasion of our coasts. The crisis saw a general embodiment of Militia ordered, in consequence of which the Anglesey Regiment assembled preparatory to proceeding on garrison duty. The embodiment took place at Llanerchymedd on the 31st March, 1778 — a date given in *The Hereford Journal* as 7th April. It is likely that the news-sheet report may well be correct, and that the 31st March was the date on which the order to embody the Corps was dated. *The Journal* goes on to say that Powder, Ball and Flints were issued to the regiment on April 25th, after which the Corps was inspected by Major General Calcraft prior to its departure for Caernarfon. The regiment remained on duty in that town until the spring of the following year.

In May, 1779, the regiment passed through Newcastle under Lyme on its route to Kent. Its destination was the great military encampment at Coxheath where it underwent regimental and Brigade training. In that month it returned by route of march to Anglesey and took up winter quarters. In 1780, on being ordered to Kent, the two locally ballotted Companies, then sum total of the regiment, and commanded by Captain Herbert Jones of Llynon, moved off immediately to join forces there assembled to resist invasion. In Anglesey meanwhile, William Peacoke, a somewhat forceful County Landowner, persuaded the then ageing and senile Lord Lieutenant, Sir Nicholas Bayley, into granting him rank in the County Militia in return for raising men for the regiment to serve in Volunteer Companies. His price for raising four Companies of 'Volunteer' Militiamen was a Lieutenant Colonelcy in the Anglesey Regiment and authority to select his own Officers. On receiving clearance to proceed with the scheme, Peacoke (likely William Peacoke of Plas yn Llanfair) selected several Irishmen, mainly friends, or their sons, to serve as Officers, none of whom were qualified by experience or by owning property within the County for such posts. Each of those selected was in return for his rank expected to raise a number of men for service. The Militiamen raised by that process were mainly Irish — dregs from that country's gaols and Poor Houses. The remainder consisted of ne'er do wells, and deserters from other Militia Regiments. With no competent Officers or Non Commissioned Officers to control them, the unruly mob were ordered to assemble at Ellesmere, and all without word or reference to Herbert Jones, the properly appointed Commandant of the regiment then on duty in Kent. On Saturday, 5th August, 1780, the following story appeared in *The Shrewsbury Chronicle:*

"Yesterday morning early, the Commanding Officer of the Worcestershire Militia quartered in this town received an express from the Officer of a Volunteer Company belonging to the Anglesey Militia quartered at Ellesmere, desiring assistance against a mutinous part of the said Company who had abused and very ill treated their Officers. The Soldiers in the above mentioned Company being Irish and Welsh, disputed about their right to take rank of one another, and all the endeavours of their Officers to command obedience proved ineffectual. Happily, they had not received arms, otherwise it is feared that much more mischief might have ensued. A Sergeant's Guard furnished with Powder and Ball were immediately sent to bring the offenders to Shrewsbury."

The rag, tag and bobtail making up the Volunteer Companies performed similarly at Oswestry where they were later quartered; the unfortunate inhabitants becoming so terrified of them as to appeal once again to the Commanding Officer of the Worcestershire Militia in Shrewsbury for protection. Into this unhappy and disgraceful situation were thrown Herbert Jones and his two balloted Companies, who on being ordered from duties in Kent to Oswestry found themselves linked with a mob of rapscallions. Even worse, Herbert Jones found himself superseded as Commanding Officer, and on refusing to serve in any lesser capacity, had no alternative but to hand over his small disciplined group to Lt Colonel Peacoke and his undisciplined rabble.

Having assured his Anglesey men that he would do all that was within his power to put matters right, Jones returned to the County to continue his fight against the injustice. Meanwhile the regiment under Peacoke rampaged its way across the border counties bringing undeserved shame to the good name of Anglesey. The worst incident took place at Kidderminster in March 1781, when the Irish Volunteers there quartered ran riot, which resulted in twenty persons being wounded and a great deal of damage to property. To their credit, not one man of the Balloted Companies was involved, but the disgrace brought upon the regiment and to their own good names obliged them to petition Lord Bulkeley, Member for Anglesey, regarding the conditions under which they were being forced to serve.

"The great injustice which we suffer, and the hardships which we bear in being joined to Mr Peacoke's Irish Volunteers and commanded by strangers is scarcely conceivable, for we are treated in a most cruel manner, insomuch that many of us are maimed and punished by our Officers without cause or trial, and we are badly cloathed, that many of us are without shoes or shirts to our backs. Notwithstanding, our Pay is stopped, and no account given us of it. All this is aggrevated by the contempt and derision the Irish treat our country and our language with. In this distressed and unhappy situation, we have none to look up to for relief but our own countrymen, and particularly your Lordship, being the representative of the County for which we serve. As such, and from your known humanity, we humbly implore your assistance to rescue us from the present situation, and to have us under Gentlemen of the County who will treat us as Soldiers.

Signed by all the Privates of the Anglesea Militia."

Their old Commanding Officer, Herbert Jones, had meanwhile not forgotten them or allowed any grass to grow under his feet. He successfully petitioned the House of Commons and forced the matter to military law. He also challenged Peacoke to a duel for being the author of libellous material against him, but as one would expect the crafty Lt Colonel managed to avoid the confrontation. Meanwhile, the regiment with its Irish Companies somewhat more orderly moved on to the Bristol Garrison and thence to Kent where in June 1781 it had detachments stationed at Folkestone, Rye and Hythe.

Towards the end of the year, Herbert Jones having won his case, the balloted Companies were ordered back to Llanerchymedd where to their delight they once more found themselves under the command of their rightful Commanding Officer. In February 1782, the Balloted Companies were disembodied and the men dismissed to their homes, whilst the Irish Volunteer Companies were marched to Winchester to await further orders. In May 1782, William Peacoke deservedly faced Court Martial, and was tried on various charges ranging from rendering false Returns to the ill treatment of Welsh Militiamen. He was found guilty and sentenced to be cashiered. By that time the 'whitewash' was out, and there were those who should have known better busy covering up on a state of affairs which should not have been allowed to continue without check for so long a period. Peacoke survived to be ordered to march his Irishmen to Holyhead where they were paid off and discharged, but their passage to Dublin had to be a matter for his own pocket. Thus ended happily an unfortunate episode in the history of the regiment, and Herbert Jones continued in command of the disembodied Corps until his retirement from Militia service in 1793.

During the next eleven years the activities of the regiment were confined to periods of annual training with numbers maintained at strength by periodic enforcement of the Ballot.

1793-1802

The outbreak of the French Revolutionary War on the 1st February, 1793, saw the Militia once again drawn out for Garrison duty.

The Anglesey Regiment, now commanded by William Evans was shortly thereafter stationed in Hampshire and had detachments on duty at Portsmouth and Forton Barracks, Gosport, where their duties were mainly connected with Dockyard Security, Coast Defence and providing escorts for the movement of Prisoners of War. In 1794 an Act of Parliament[2] authorised an augmentation of the Militia, and that resulted in an extra Company of 84 men being raised and later added to the regiment.

The 20th February, 1795, saw a change of Commanding Officers when Major George Arthur Paget succeeded William Evans to command the Corps then numbering two Companies. *The Hereford Journal* records Liverpool as a regimental station in 1788 where it was possibly standing by to proceed on Irish service. No record of any movement to, or activities in that country, has been found, but it is known that several Welsh Militia regiments served there during and after the rebellion of that year.

The continued threat of invasion caused Government to increase the size of the Militia Force, the various regiments at that time being strengthened by additional Companies of Supplementary Militia. A proportion of the additional men drawn out by the scheme[3] were allowed the option of volunteering to serve with the Regular Army, and many accepted. In that manner the Militia commenced to act as an useful reserve for the Regular Land Forces of the Crown. The Anglesey Regiment was now somewhat larger, the quota for the County being in 1796 set at 320.

By 1802 the regiment had returned to Anglesey, where with hostilities temporarily ended due to the signing of the Peace of Amiens in March, the Corps stood down, and the men were dismissed to their homes.

1803-1815

In May 1803, the short lived peace foundered as Britain declared War on Napoleonic France. The renewal of hostilities saw the regiment drawn out for the longest embodiment in its history, a period which is undoubtedly the high point in the annals of the Corps.

The regiment at that date commanded by Major William Lewis Hughes was reported in the *Cambrian* of that month as "Marching towards the coast", presumably the South Coast of England where the anti-invasion forces were concentrating.

With the military might of Napoleonic France directed against her, the situation in Britain was in many ways similar to that of 1940, when our country stood alone facing the armed might of Nazi Germany. That the invasion threat was real, is confirmed by the words of a pamphlet, presumably intended for circulation amongst French troops who were to follow the initial assault, a translation of which was published in the *Cambrian* — "French Republic, Army of England.

"The sea is passed, the boundaries of nature have yielded to the genius and fortune of the Hero, the Saviour of France; and haughty England already groans under the yoke of her Conquerors. London is before you! that Peru of the old world is your prey. Within twenty days I plant the Tricolour Flag on the once proud walls of her execrable Tower. March! the road to Victory is open."

On the 9th March, 1804, the same news-sheet warned its readers — "It is generally believed that the period of invasion is now not too far distant. We should constantly be prepared to the fullest extent possible, and we have no doubt that Cambria's loyal Sons will be found amongst the foremost in the hour of danger, not only to meet and repulse the enemy, but to furnish every requiste, assistance of Waggons, etc, to their Brothers in Arms." 1804 saw the regiment granted the privilege of using the prefix 'Royal' in its title and as such be entitled to wear the Royal Blue facings of such regiments.

The Victory at Trafalgar in October 1805 removed for the duration the threat of invasion, the Anglesey regiment at that date occupying itself on duties in the South Eastern counties. In early May 1808 the Corps marched out of Norwich en route for Chatham. In August of that same year when stationed at Margate under the command of Lt Colonel W.L. Hughes, the regiment volunteered for active service in Spain and Portugal — an offer, which although greatly appreciated, was politely declined, as were also the services of other similarly inclined regiments of Militia. Details of the offer were published in *The North Wales Gazette* in September and also in the South Wales news-sheet, *Cambrian*.

"To the Editors of the North Wales Gazette,
Gentlemen,

The pleasure with which the Royal Anglesey Regiment at all times received your paper was much increased on the receipt of that of the 18th inst, containing that loyal, manly and truly British address voted by the County to His Majesty at the meeting in Llangefni on the 12th, Birthday of the Prince of Wales — an address which animated every man in the regiment, and on the 24th, their ensuing muster day, they all stepped forward, and with one voice, offered their services in so glorious a cause. I send you a copy of our gallant Colonel's Regimental Orders on the day following, and am.

Sir,
Your most obedient Servant,
H. Jones,
Sergeant Major to Royal Anglesey Fusileers
(Margate Barracks, Aug. 26th, 1808)

The Copy
Sir,

I am desired by the Officers, Non Commissioned Officers and Privates of the Royal Anglesey Militia under my command to express the lively interest which they feel in the glorious cause which animates the Spaniards, and their most anxious wish personally to contribute to its success; in testimony of which I am to report their readiness to embark for Spain whenever His Majesty may be graciously pleased to accept their services. I request you will communicate to His Royal Highness, the Commander in Chief, this unanimous and voluntary offer of the Corps to extend its service.

I have the honour to be, Sir,
etc, etc,
W.L. Hughes, Colonel Commandant
Royal Anglesey Militia or Fusileers
To the Adjutant General of the Forces
Margate August 25th, 1808."

In July 1809, the Royal Anglesey moved from Margate to Ospringe Barracks, near Faversham, and in August to Deal. The Corps was at this date short on its establishment due to the loss of men who had volunteered for service with the Line, and an adjustment of the Militia quota. A deadline of October 10th was set, by which date it was expected to complete the required numbers. The early months of 1811 found the regiment stationed at Eastbourne which town it quitted at the end of June to take up duties in Langney Point Barracks. Later in the year it embarked for Ireland and was stationed at Omagh, Co Tyrone. It remained in that country until June 1813, when it marched in to Dublin in preparation for its return to the mainland. ***The Cambrian*** reporting its imminent return said, "The Royal Anglesea Light Infantry Regiment of Militia under Captain Mitchell marched into Dublin on Saturday the 15th ult from Downpatrick. They are to embark for Liverpool in a few days. At a Meeting of the Gentlemen and Magistrates of Downpatrick on the 9th ult, an address was presented to Captain Mitchell which concludes thus: 'During a period of upwards of 15 months during which the regiment has been quartered here. We have witnessed the most gentlemanly conduct of the Officers, and the most orderly and soldierlike demenour of the Non-

Commissioned Officers and Privates, and we have only to assure you, Captain Mitchell, that the regiment carries with it our most sincere wishes for its prosperity and happiness!"

This was tribute indeed, particularly coming from the inhabitants of a country, which then, as in Ulster of the present day, was no 'picnic spot' for the troops selected as garrison. It also questions the far too widely held belief that Militiamen were for the most part an unruly and poor disciplined arm of the military.

From Liverpool later that month, the regiment marched down to Bristol, which garrison they quitted in mid July on being ordered to duties in Nottingham. As far as is known that remained as its station until June 1814, by which date Napoleon had abdicated and a Treaty of Peace had been signed.

Circular Letter No.230 dated 16th June, 1814, authorised the disembodiment of the Militia — "His Royal Highness, the Prince Regent, having been pleased in the name of, and on behalf of His Majesty, to sign Orders for the disembodying of the Militia of the County of 'Anglesea' with all convenient speed, etc, etc."

Later in the month *The Cambrian* reported its return to the County, "The Anglesey, Flint, Carnarvon and Montgomery Regiments arrived in their native counties last week where they were received with loud and reiterated cheers after their long and arduous service."

In July 1814 the regiment stood down, and was disembodied at Beaumaris on completion of over eleven years of continuous service.

On standing down, each Private man received his pay in full, and was allowed to keep his regimental clothing and knapsnack. On parade, prior to dismissal, messages of thanks from both the King and Parliament were read out to them, e.g.,

"Die Martis, 5th July, 1814.

"Resolved nemine dissintentie, by the Lords Spiritual and Temporal in Parliament assembled, that this House do highly approve and acknowledge the service of the Non Commissioned Officers and Men of the several Corps of Militia which have been embodied in Great Britain and Ireland during the course of the War, and that the same be communicated to them by the Commanding Officers of the several Corps, who are desired to thank them for their meritorious conduct."

1815-1852

The end of the Napoleonic Wars saw the Militia of the Kindgom enter into a long period of decline and inactivity, a state of affairs not uncommon after the conclusion of a successful War. An Act of 1816 allowed Government to suspend Militia training, and in consequence the regiment, like those of the other Welsh Counties, although kept up to strength by ballot, was not drawn out for training until 1820. Similar training periods took place in 1821 and

1825. The next, in 1831 which extended over a period of 28 days was to be the last for twenty two years, as the Militia was not called out again until 1853.

During that period, the regiment, like others, was reduced to little more than a name in the Army List, and although Officers continued to be appointed, the suspension of the Militia Ballot gave them no men to command. All that remained to remind the public of the existence of the regiment was an Adjutant with one or two Staff Instructors manning the County Militia Headquarters and with very little work of a military nature to justify their appointments. In 1852, the Force was revived, and in that year a much increased Permanent Staff set about recruiting Volunteers for the regiment in preparation for Militia training in the following year.

The Militia Ballot meanwhile remained suspended, with the proviso that it could be reintroduced if the numbers required could not be obtained by voluntary enlistment.

Under the terms of the Militia Act of 1852, men offering their services were to serve for five years, and on attestment would receive a Cash Bounty. Training periods in the first instance would be for twenty-one days annually, which period could be increased if required to 56 days by an Order in Council.

The year 1852 saw the death of William Lewis Hughes who had commanded the Corps during the 'Long Embodiment'. Created Lord Dinorben in 1831, he was succeeded as Commanding Officer by Thomas Peers Williams of Craig y Don in the County.

1853-1876

Revived as the 'Royal Anglesey Rifle Corps', the regiment was drawn out for training in 1853, but the Rifles role was to be short lived, and brought little change as the regiment reverted to the old Light Infantry role during that same year. Annual training continued uninterrupted, and apart from a short embodiment during the Crimean War crisis in 1855, the history of the regiment up to that date was fairly uneventful.

During the Crimean embodiment which ended on May 31st, 1856, the Corps produced several Volunteers for service with the Line, but its activities were confined to training at Beaumaris where the men were billeted in public houses and lodging houses across the town.

A reorganisation of 1860 saw the Anglesey Regiment united with that of neighbouring Caernarfonshire under the title 'Royal Carnarvon and Anglesey Rifles' and a change from the Light Infantry to the Rifles role. The authority for this change was given in a War Office Letter dated 28th July, 1860,[4] and such evidence as exists suggests that both the Anglesey and Caernarfonshire contingents trained together during the amalgamation period. Venue for training between 1860 and 1866 was Caernarfon, but to avoid repetition, additional information on the activities of the united Corps will be found in that section of this work which deals with the history of the Caernarfonshire

Militia. On the 11th March, 1867, authorisation was received for the separation of the Militia of the two Counties, at which point the Anglesey contingent regained independent status under its old title of 'Royal Anglesey Light Infantry Militia'.

1877-1908

In pursuance of Government policy to provide the Militia Force with its own Corps of Artillery and Engineers, the Royal Anglesey in 1877 found itself selected in company with the Royal Monmouth to convert to the Military Engineers role. The change took place on April 1st, 1877, on which date it was redesignated as the 'Royal Anglesey Engineers Militia'. Headquarters of the regiment remained at Beaumaris, and its precedence number in the roll of Engineer Militia Regiments nationally was '2'.

In its new role, the regiment still received a certain amount of basic Infantry and Musketry training, but as Engineers, the main efforts annually were directed towards perfection in the construction of fortifications, sapping, mining and bridgebuilding. By 1900 it had also extended into the field of railway maintenance, and recruited, not only in Anglesey, but also throughout all of the North Wales counties.

Embodied for service on the 7th May, 1900, the regiment then consisted of two Field Companies drawn from Anglesey and four Sub Divisions each provided by Caernarfonshire, Meirionethshire, Flintshire and Denbighshire.

Although the whole regiment volunteered for service with the Regular Army in South Africa, its services en masse in that campaign were not required. Instead, selected groups of Volunteers were drawn out and formed into Service Detachments, the first of which, known as the First Service Detachment, consisting of 25 Non Commissioned Officers and Men under the command of Captain J.L. Hampton Lewis, embarked for the Cape on the 6th March, 1900. On arrival in South Africa they were attached to 'A' Pontoon Troop, Royal Engineers, where in addition to work of that nature they gave a good account of themselves in repairing the Railway between Ladysmith and Standerton, as also in clearing the Laings Nek Tunnel. They returned home in June 1901, and were replaced by a regimental group known as 'A' Company which consisted of three Officers, 103 Other Ranks under the command of Captain (Hon Major) F.H. Rawlins. This Company embarked for the Cape on June 6th, 1900, and were stationed at Kimberley in which district they were employed on Railway repairs and Blockhouse construction. A Detachment of the Company was also present at the Siege of Schweitzer Renecke during the latter part of that eventful year. The Company came home in October 1901. During the campaign two Sappers died, and whilst others were touched by fever, the regiment on the whole suffered very lightly.

The passing of the Territorial and Reserve Forces Act of 1907 resulted in the Militia ceasing to be raised in the United Kingdom. In April 1908 those members of the old regiment who had elected to continue in service were transferred to the Special Reserve under the title 'Royal Anglesey Royal Engineers (S.R.)'.

Under that title it rendered valuable service through until 1919, but the 20s of this century finally saw it fade away into obscurity.

Footnotes

1. Clwyd Record Office. D/GA/1090
2. Act 34 Geo 111.c.36
3. Supplementary Militia Act. 26 Geo 11.c.107
4. Records 4th Bn, Royal Welsh Fusiliers

Other Sources
The Cambrian
The North Wales Gazette

LIST OF OFFICERS

May 1779

Captain Herbert Jones of Llynon, Captain Commandant	26.3.1778
Lieut. Edward Bailie	26.3.1778
Ensign Stephen Price (also Adjutant)	26.3.1778
Q.M. Williams Peters	
Surgeon Thomas Pidgeon	

May 1781

Lieut. Colonel Commandant William Peacocke	28.2.1781
Major George Irwine	30.3.1781
Captain Kilner Baker	28.2.1781
Captain Edward Baillie	30.3.1781
Captain Lieutenant John Griffith	30.3.1781
Lieut. George Whiteway	28.2.1781
Lieut. William Graham	28.2.1781
Lieut. Graves Chamney	28.2.1781
Lieut. Daniel Maroney	30.3.1781
Ensign John Sheppard	28.2.1781
Ensign Thomas Parker	28.2.1781
Ensign William Bourke	28.2.1781
Ensign Richard Bourke	30.3.1781
Ensign W. Ridout (Adjutant)	25.4.1780
QM William Peters	2.4.1778
Surgeon Thomas Pidgeon	2.4.1778

Corps Agents — Messrs Fitter & Croasdaile, Gt Pultney St, Golden Square, London.

1793

Captain Commandant William Evans	23.1.1793
Lieut. Bodychan Sparrow	4.9.1793
QM Thomas O'Neill	5.9.1792

1795

Major Commandant Hon Arthur Paget	20.2.1795
Captain William Lewis Hughes	14.11.1794
Lieut. and Adjutant Bodychan Sparrow	4.9.1793
Agents — Mr Fenwick, Millbank St, London	

1800

Lieut. Colonel Cdt Hon Arthur Paget	10.3.1798
Captain John Bodychan Sparrow	4.4.1797
Captain John Griffith Lewis	8.6.1798
Lieut. Bodychan Sparrow (Adjutant) & (QM)	4.9.1793
Lieut. William Bodychan Parry	1.2.1798
Lieut. William Jones	1.2.1798
Ensign Henry Byne	10.8.1798
Ensign J. Pritchard	24.8.1798
Ensign J. Pike	24.8.1798
Surgeon Griffith Jones	2.4.1795

1803 (July)

Major Cdt William Lewis Hughes	18.4.1803
Captain John Bodychan Sparrow	4.4.1798
Lieut. Richard Griffith Jones	1.11.1798
Lieut. John Pike	18.4.1803
Ensign Henry Byne	10.8.1798
Lieut. Bodychan Sparrow (Adjutant)	
Surgeon John Pritchard	

April 1808

Lieut. Colonel W.L. Hughes	28.6.1803
Captain Thomas Mitchell	4.8.1803
Captain John Pike	30.7.1804
Captain John Dutton (Adjutant)	26.12.1804
1st Lieut. A. Walker	28.6.1803
1st Lieut. T. Gray	28.11.1803
2nd Lieut. H. Byne (also Paymaster)	10.8.1798
2nd Lieut. N. Byne	25.4.1804
Surgeon J. Pritchard	

August 1811

Major Commandant Colonel W.L. Hughes	
Captain T. Mitchell	4.8.1803
1st Lieut. Anthony Walker	28.6.1803
1st Lieut. Thomas Grey	28.11.1803
2nd Lieut. Henry Byne	10.8.1798 (Paymaster)

2nd Lieut. H. Horton	1.6.1811
Captain John Kirsopp (Adjutant)	3.4.1809
Surgeon John Pritchard	10.8.1798

August 1814

Major Commandant Colonel W.L. Hughes	
Captain Thomas Mitchell	
1st Lieut. Anthony Walker	
2nd Lieut. John Haston	1.6.1811
Adjutant Henry Jones	11.2.1812
Surgeon J. Pritchard	

January 1815 Colonels and Permanent Staff, Disembodied Militia

Major Commandant Colonel William Lewis Hughes
Adjutant Henry Jones
Surgeon John Pritchard

September 1820

Major Commandant Colonel William Lewis Hughes	
Captain Thomas Mitchell	
1st Lieut. Thomas Grey	
1st Lieut. Thomas P. Williams	3.4.1819
2nd Lieut. John Harton	1.6.1811
2nd Lieut. Henry Jones	3.4.1819
Paymaster Thomas Grey	
Adjutant Henry Grotty	3.4.1819
Surgeon John Pritchard	

September 1825

Major Commandant Colonel William Lewis Hughes	
Captain Thomas Pierce Williams	30.4.1825
1st Lieut. and Paymaster Thomas Grey	
1st Lieut. Richard Bulkeley Williams	30.4.1825
2nd Lieut. John Harton	
2nd Lieut. Henry Jones	
Adjutant Henry Grotty	
Surgeon Edward Snow	

1853

Colonel Thomas Peers Williams
Captain John Lewis Hampton Lewis (late 5th Dragoon Guards)
Captain Charles Stanmore Jones (late 59th Regt)
Captain Richard Trygarn Griffiths
Lieut. Thomas Love Duncome Jones Parry

Lieut. John Thomas Roberts
Lieut. Henry Robert Poole
Ensign Owen Lewis Cope Williams
Ensign Stephen Roose
Ensign Eyre Lloyd
Captain & Adjutant Septimus A. Cary (late 31st Regt)
Surgeon Robert Wynne Jones

1861

Hon. Colonel Hon. Edward Gordon Douglas Pennant (late Grenadier Guards)	30.8.1852
Lieut. Colonel Cdt Thomas Peers Williams	
Captain John Lewis Hampton Lewis	
Captain T.L.D. Jones Parry	29.5.1854
Captain John Thomas Roberts, J.P.	5.10.1855
Lieut. Henry Owen Williams	26.3.1859
Lieut. William Henry Copeland	11.10.1860
Lieut. Alfred Theodore Williams	11.10.1860
Captain & Adjutant E.W. Pearse (Lieut. half pay. R.M. Artillery)	21.7.1858
Surgeon Walter Humphries, MD.	1.11.1855
Agents — Cox & Co.	

September 1881

Lieut. Colonel T.L. Hampton Lewis
Captain R.H.B. Galbraith
Captain W.D. Lloyd
Captain L.F. Dwyer
Lieut. R.E.W. Isaacson
Lieut. R.H.W. Bulkeley
Lieut. L.O. Williams
Lieut. J.L. Rowley
Major J.A. Hepper, RE. (Adjutant)
Medical Officer W. Humphries, MD.

1885

Lieut. Colonel T.L. Hampton Lewis	14.8.1873
Captain R.H.R. Galbraith	16.6.1871
Captain L.F.W. Dwyer	3.12.1877
Captain R. ap H. Williams	20.4.1884
Lieut. W.G. Massey	7.7.1883
Lieut. G.H. Lambert	19.7.1884
Hon. Colonel T.L. Hampton Lewis	17.10.1891
Lieut. Colonel Sir R.H. Williams Bulkeley, Bt.	10.2.1897

Major C. Mathews Donaldson	12.5.1899
Major F. Boynton	1.5.1900
Captain F.H. Rawlins	12.11.1892
Captain T.F. Evans	1.4.1895
Captain J.H. Pritchard Rayner	10.3.1897
Captain Sir T.L.H. Neave, Bt	9.5.1898
Lieut. L.H.G. Lloyd	29.3.1899
Lieut. L. Hepworth	4.4.1900
Lieut. A.L. Stanley	16.5.1900
Lieut. A.H. Vivian	16.5.1900
2nd Lieut. G.C. Harvey	28.3.1900
2nd Lieut. W.H. Pery Knox Gore	8.4.1900
2nd Lieut. A.F.G. Pery Knox Gore	8.4.1900
2nd Lieut. G.W.B. Copeman	19.4.1900
2nd Lieut. W.S. Phelan	3.5.1900
2nd Lieut. C.E. Hatchell	13.6.1900
2nd Lieut. J.R.M. Mathews Donaldson	23.6.1900
2nd Lieut. R.K. McClymont	18.7.1900
Captain C.C.J. Pery (Adjutant) RE.	1.4.1897

February 1908

Hon. Colonel T.L. Hampton Lewis	17.10.1891
Lieut. Colonel C. Mathews Donaldson	18.10.1905
Major F. Beynton	1.5.1900
Major H.B.L. Hughes	24.1.1901
Major R.V. Jellicoe	29.11.1905
Major G.C. Harvey	12.11.1907
Captain D.O. Springfield	27.5.1903
Captain E. Thew	12.7.1903
Captain R.K. McClymont	6.10.1906
Captain G.A. Jones	12.11.1907
Lieut. C.E. Wilson	21.3.1903
Lieut. R. Williams	21.3.1903
Lieut. M. Parrington	23.12.1905
Lieut. B.M.B.H. Gyll Murray	14.5.1907
Lieut. E.U. Grimshaw	15.5.1907
Lieut. The Hon. M.H.E.C. Townley Bertie	27.6.1907
Captain G.A. Jones (Inst. of Musketry)	15.3.1907
Captain F.A.K. White, RE. Adjutant	2.10.1907
Hon. Lieut. W.T. Basley, RE. QM	

THOMAS GRIFFITHS — Late, The Anglesey Militia

Thomas Griffiths served with the County Militia as a Drummer from May 24th, 1793, to 13th September, 1807.

Born in Caernarfon, and a Shoemaker by trade, in 1807 he volunteered to serve with the Line and was attested in the 23rd Foot, Royal Welch Fusiliers on the 13th September at the given age of 28.

Promoted Corporal on March 25th, 1808, and Drum Major on the 25th September, 1810, he was present with the Grenadier Company of the 23rd on the Field of Waterloo.

His date of discharge from the Army is not known, but he died on the 13th September, 1854, aged 88, and was buried at Llanelly Churchyard, Gilwern, near Abergavenny, Monmouthshire.

His age at death is said to have been 88, but if Army Records are correct, his true age on demise was 75.

UNIFORM DRESS

The Uniform Dress of both Officers and Other Ranks was up to 1877 similar in design to that worn by the Infantry of the Line. Red/Scarlet with Blue Facings with Loops, white and in pairs, are recorded by J. Osborn, c.1780. Hamilton Smith in 1814 records Red with Blue Facings. No change is recorded for the period 1815 to 1860; but that year saw unification with the Carnarvon Quota and in due course the old style uniform was discarded for Rifle Green with Red Facings. In 1867 the regiment once again took up the Light Infantry role, and one presumes that it once again adopted the Scarlet Coat. This is supported by the Army List of November 1869 which shows the regiment to be wearing Blue Facings.

On conversion to Engineers Militia in 1877, the regiment in due course adopted the style and pattern worn by the Royal Engineers, i.e., Red with Blue Facings and with Militia distinctions.

COLOURS

A King's or First Colour and Regimental or Second Colour was carried by the regiment from 1762 through until 1877 apart from the period 1852-1867 when the regiment served in the Rifles role. The Colours, c.1763, consisted of the King's Colour — a large Union Flag 6′ on the pole and 6′6″ in the fly, and a Regimental Colour of similar dimensions having at its centre, painted or embroidered on the silk, the Arms of the Lord Lieutenant of the County.

C.1804, a new King's Colour was taken into use, consisting of a large Union of similar dimensions to its predecessor. The Regimental Colour was however changed, and although of similar dimensions to that which it replaced incorporated the Plumes, Coronet and Motto of the Prince of Wales and the Regimental Title.

Neither Colour appears to have survived the passage of time, but sometime post 1877 passed into the hands of either the Colonel of the Regiment or an Anglesey Parish Church.

BADGES AND BUTTONS

ROYAL ANGLESEY LIGHT INFANTRY MILITIA
SHAKO PLATE. OFFICERS PATT. c.1854
(Owen Collection)

ROYAL ANGLESEY LIGHT INFANTRY MILITIA SHAKO PLATE, OFFICERS PATTERN, c.1854

A silver cut Star surmounted by a gilt Victorian Crown. Superimposed upon the star backplate, a Garter Belt within a wreath of Laurels, all in gilt and surmounted by a gilt crown with red plush velvet cushions. The garter belt is fretted to show the title 'Royal Anglesey Light Inf' on a Royal Blue enamel ground. Inside the belt, the Plumes, Coronet and Motto of the Prince of Wales in silver on a Royal Blue ground. Pendant below the central device, a gilded stringed Bugle Horn of the Light Infantry pattern.

This handsome Shako Plate was worn from 1844 on the first Albert pattern Shako, and quite likely on its Bell topped predecessor. I also believe, that the Plate, minus its Victorian Crown, was the design worn by Officers of the Corps on the Regency Pattern Shako. Another version of this Plate was once held on which the Prince of Wales's badge at the centre had a gilded Coronet and Motto Scrolls. An example of the Plate may be seen in the Royal Welch Fusiliers Museum.

ROYAL ANGLESEY LIGHT INFANTRY MILITIA
SHOULDER BELT PLATE. OFFICERS PATTERN, c.1854
By kind permission of Dr J. Carey Hughes

ROYAL ANGLESEY LIGHT INFANTRY SHOULDER BELT PLATE. OFFICERS PATT, c.1854

An oblong silver Plate having superimposed on its face a device consisting of a Garter Belt and Crown in gilt, the belt inscribed in raised letters with the title 'ROYAL ANGLESEY LIGHT INFANTRY'. Inside the belt on a burnished silver ground, and in frosted silver, the Plumes, Coronet and Motto of the Prince of Wales. Pendant below the Garter Belt, a gilt stringed Bugle Horn of the Light Infantry pattern.

Parkyn describes a similar Plate which once formed part of the late Mr Usher's Collection. On that Plate, the badge of the Prince of Wales has a gilt coronet.

The Plate was worn by Officers of the Corps between 1844 and 1855. An example of the type can be seen in the Royal Welch Fusiliers Museum.

ROYAL ANGLESEY LIGHT INFANTRY MILITIA
WAIST BELT CLASP. OFFICERS PATTERN, c.1855
A Locket pattern Clasp in silver plated metal with the Plumes, Coronet and Motto Scrolls and Pendant Bugle Horn in silver on frosted silver ground.
(Owen Collection)

BUTTON. WHITE METAL. OTHER RANKS PATT
ROYAL ANGLESEY LIGHT INFANTRY MILITIA, c.1855
(Owen Collection)

TOP
BADGE. OTHER RANKS PATTERN FOR WEAR ON GLENGARRY CAP, c.1875
Superimposed across the strings of a Light Infantry pattern Bugle Horn, A Druid's Head flanked by sprays of Oak Leaf and Acorn, the whole in Brass.

BOTTOM
BUTTON. OFFICERS TUNIC PATT, c.1868
Silver, convex and closed back with a design consisting of the Bugle Horn pendant below the Plumes, Coronet and Motto of the Prince of Wales, the whole enclosed by the regimental title. Parkyn states that the silver Coatee Button worn by Officers of the Corps, pre 1855 carried a similar design on the face.
(Owen Collection)

ROYAL ANGLESEY ENGINEERS MILITIA WAIST BELT CLASP. OFFICERS PATTERN, c.1880

A silver oblong plate with rounded corners. Superimposed on its face the gilt device of a Druid's Head flanked with sprays of Oak Leaf and Acorn. Above the head, the Plumes, Coronet and Motto of the Prince of Wales, and below, a three part scroll inscribed 'MÔN MAM CYMRU' (Mona Mother of Wales)

A similar Belt Clasp, the whole in silver plate, and another consisting of a gilt back plate with silver device exists.

Note: It has been said that the device carried on this Plate was worn by Officers on the Undress Forage Cap — a badge of embroidered construction. No record, documentary or photographic, has been found which would support that claim.

ROYAL ANGLESEY ENGINEERS MILITIA
(Owen Collection)

WAIST BELT CLASP, DEVICE AND CLASP, OFFICERS PATTERN, c.1880
(Owen Collection)

Examples of General Pattern Helmet Plates worn by Militia Engineers on the Home Service Blue Cloth Helmet during the period 1878 to 1902
Courtesy of H.L. King

General Pattern Helmet Plates, Royal Engineers Militia for wear on Home Service Blue Cloth Helmet 1902-1908 and Forage Cap, Cap Badge for the same period.
Courtesy H.L. King

CARNARVONSHIRE MILITIA

1762 The Carnarvonshire Militia
1800 Royal Carnarvon Fuzileers
1804 Royal Carnarvonshire Militia
1810 Royal Carnarvonshire Light Infantry
1812 Royal Carnarvon (Rifle Corps)
1860 Royal Carnarvon and Anglesey Rifles
1867 Royal Carnarvon Rifle Corps
1881 4th Battalion, The Royal Welsh Fusiliers
1908 Disbanded

Precedence Numbers

1803 16
1833 56

Commanding Officers

1762 Thomas Wynne of Glynllifon (later Lord Newborough)
1781 Ellis Wynne
1793 Richard Edwards
1838 Major O.C.J. Nanney
1852 Hon. Edward Gordon Douglas Pennant
1858 John McDonald
1865 Lieut. Colonel H.M. Jones
1884 Lieut. Colonel H. Platt
1899 Lieut. Colonel O.L.J. Evans
1903 Lieut. Colonel H.R.H. Lloyd-Mostyn

Under the terms of the Militia Act of 1757, the County was required to provide 80 men to serve on its behalf in a regiment of Militia. The provision of the men presented no great problem, but the Lord Lieutenant found some difficulty in raising Officers. An attempt was made to comply with the Act in 1758, but failed due to the lack of sufficient numbers of suitably qualified gentlemen of the County expressing willingness to serve as Officers in the Corps.

1762-1763

The Regiment was eventually raised in 1762, the Order for its embodiment being included in an interesting article which appeared in *Y Cymmrodor* 1935,[1] as also in the Records of the 4th Royal Welsh Fusiliers.

"An Order to embody the County Militia signed by George Grenville Secretary of State, Northern Department.
George R.
Our late Royal Grandfather of glorious and happy memory having (agreeably to the Acts for the better ordering of the Militia Forces in that part of Great Britain called England) communicated to Parliament that he has received repeated intelligence of the actual preparations making in the French Ports to invade this Kingdom, and of the imminent danger of such invasion being attempted, and the apprehension of such a design on the part of France not yet being removed; Our Will and Pleasure is, and We do hereby Order you, with all convenient speed, to draw out and embody, at such place as you shall judge most convenient, all the Militia of the County of Carnarvon under your direction, and that you do cause the same to be held in every respect, ready to march as occasion shall require, to such posts within this Kingdom as We shall judge proper to assign them, and to put under the command of such General Officer or Officers as We shall be pleased to appoint over them, and to obey such further Orders as shall be judged necessary for the safety and defence of these Kingdoms, and for doing so, this shall be your Warrant. Given at Our Court of St. James's, the twenty eighth day of September, 1762, in the Second Year of Our Reign.
By His Majesty's Command
George Grenville
To Our Trusty and Well Beloved Thomas Wynne, Esq.
Our Lieutenant of Our County of Carnarvon and (in his absence) to the Deputy Lieutenants of Our said County."

Although the Order is dated 28th September, the actual embodiment did not take place until the 5th October. The venue was Caernarfon, where the small regiment was immediately put under training, Arms having been received on the 28th August.

As far as is known, the regiment did not move out of the county; the men being dismissed to their homes on completion of training early in the following year.

1764-1777

During this period the regiment was kept up to strength by enforcement of the ballot and presumably, as required by law, drawn out periodically for training. A weekly Return preserved in the Records of the 4th Bn, Royal Welsh Fusiliers, shows that Arms and Stores of the Royal Carnarvonshire Grenadiers were stored at Fort Williamsburg, Glynllifon. One writer[2] suggests that the Royal Carnarvon Grenadiers was but another name for Lord Newborough's private Corps — The Garrison of Fort Williamsburg; but a study of the Arms and Equipment listed in the Return show that the amount compares very favourably with the strength of the County Militia, the quota for which was 80 men. It is also highly unlikely that Lord Newborough would be required to account to Government for material which was his personal and private property.

Weekly Return of Arms and Stores — 31st October, 1773

4 Espontoons
2 Colour Cases
80 Firelocks
80 Bayonets
80 Cartouche Boxes
86 Hangers
80 Pouches
83 Buff Belts
83 Brown Belts
80 Slings
12 Light Field Locks
12 Bayonets
2 Light Horsemen's Pouches
2 Light Horsemen's Swords
2 Light Horsemen's Caps
6 Musikmen's Swords
17 Turnscrews
11 Worms
4 Iron Scrapers
4 Sergeants' Sashes
2 Prickers
1 Iron Swivel
2 Brass Swivels
78 Privates Caps
2 Pioneers Caps
6 Drum Cases
6 French Horns
2 Clarinets
1 Tabor Pipe
2 Shoulder Belts for Pioneers
80 Flints
80 Hammer Caps
17 Prs White Gaiters
73 Prs Brown Gaiters
2 Prs Stockings
60 Stocks and Clasps
80 Buckles and Garters
16 Spare Clasps
12 Spare Buckles
12 Spare Gaiters
1 Dining Tent
5 Officers' Tents
23 Privates' Tents
6 Coarse Stools
14 Camp Stools
3 Hampers of Canteens and Kettles
1 Speaking Trumpet
1 Sword
4 Sergeants' Caps
4 Drummers' Caps
2 Fifers' Caps
6 Camp Tables
1 Dining Table
1 Officers' Old Tent
1 Servants' Tent
3 Bales Barrack Bedding
1 Mat for Dining Tent
3 Bell Tents
2 Suits of Clothes for Light Horsemen
13 Suits of Clothes for Private Men
13½ Barrels of Powder
6 Cannons and Carriage
1 Brass Blunderbuss
2 Flagstaffs
1 Box and Pole
1 Large Gun
1 Colour Box
25 Camp Blankets
5 Mats for Officers
49 Privates' Mats
4 Suits of Clothes for Musik Men
2 Powder Cases
2 Field Pieces and Carriages
3 St. George Flags

Signed: Walter Conarly (Connelly?)
Sergeant Major

1778-1783

The War with France saw the regiment embodied for service, the order of embodiment being worded as follows:

"George R.

We having (agreeably to the Acts for the better ordering of the Militia Forces in that part of Great Britain called England) communicated to Parliament Our having received advice that the warlike preparations in France become every day more considerable, and that in this critical conjecture, We feel for Our Faithful People, if We ommited any means in Our power that might contribute to their Defence. Our Will and Pleasure is, and We do hereby Order you with all convenient speed to draw out and embody, at such place as you shall judge most convenient, all the Militia of the County of Carnarvon under your direction, and that you do cause the same to be held in every respect ready to march as occasion shall require to such Posts within the Kingdom as We shall judge proper to assign them, and to be put under the command of such General Officer or Officers as We shall be pleased to appoint over them, and to obey such further Orders as shall be judged necessary for the safety and defence of the Kingdom, and for so doing, this shall be your Warrant. Given at Our Court at St. James's, the 26th Day of March, 1778, in the Eighteenth Year of our Reign.'"[2]

The document, signed by Lord Weymouth was addressed to "Our Right Trusty and Wellbeloved, Thomas, Lord Newborough, Our Lieutenant of Our County of Carnarvon, and in his absence, to the Deputy Lieutenants of the County."

After the embodiment, the regiment marched to Holyhead and was there employed on Garrison duties until the Spring of the following year. By June 1799, the regiment was serving in Kent, where encamped with other units at Coxheath it underwent a period of regimental and Brigade training. In 1782 it moved on to take up duties in Essex and there remained until the end of hostilities in 1783. It then marched back to Caernarfon and was disembodied.

1793-1801

Embodied again in 1793 due to the French declaration of War on Great Britain, the Carnarvonshire Regiment marched down to the South Coast of England and there joined other units gathered to meet the threat of invasion. Its Headquarters for a period was located at Eastbourne, but it later moved on into Kent where several of its members had served during the previous War. The continued threat to our coasts saw the Militia strengthened, the Caernarfonshire Quota being increased to 176 in 1796 and in 1799 to 239. The Ballot system was extremely unpopular in the County, partly due to the substitute system which allowed the better off to buy their way out of their national service obligation, and also due to the burden thrown onto parishes of supporting financially the families of those selected to serve. Demonstrations and protest meetings took place at Penmachno, Dolwyddelan, Ysbyty Ifan and

Capel Curig, whilst at Cerrig y Drudion, a balloted man was snatched from the hands of the military by protesters.[4]

In 1802, the signing of the Peace of Amiens brought hostilities to an end, and the regiment was in due course marched back to the County and disembodied.

1803-1814

The renewal of hostilities in 1803 saw the regiment embodied and by June it was once again serving on the, by now, familiar South Coast. By 1806 it had moved to the West Country and was stationed at New Cranby Barracks, Plymouth Dock, nowadays better known as Devonport. There it was much involved with Dockyard Security, Coast Defence, and the guarding of Prisoners of War confined to the Hulks or in the notorious Mill Prison.

On February 1st, 1808, a detachment of Militiamen newly raised to bring the regiment up to strength marched out from Bangor to join the main body at Plymouth,[5] and in May of that same year the Royal Carnarvon moved on to Sussex to take up duties at Chichester and Worthing. Whilst serving in that County, the regiment volunteered to serve in Ireland, an offer which so moved a Major Roland of the Royal Staffordshire Militia that he gave 10 Guineas to the men of the Royal Carnarvon for their entertainment and to mark his approval of their expression of loyalty. Moving on, the regiment also served at Battle and Winchelsea in 1808, but by March 1809 were stationed at Pevensey Barracks. It later moved on to Hythe and then Worthing before embarking at Portsmouth for Ireland where in November 1810 it was stationed at Longford. During the whole of this period the regiment provided a steady stream of volunteers for service with the regiments of the Line.

Whilst at Longford, the regiment volunteered for active service with Wellington's army in the Peninsula. This patriotic offer was reported in *The Cambrian* on December 18th, 1810.

"The Royal Carnarvon Militia have volunteered their services to serve in Spain and Portugal, which offer was transmitted through the Lord Lieutenant of the County to Lord Bathurst, by whom it was laid before His Royal Highness, The Prince Regent, who was pleased to express himself highly gratified with the manner in which that distinguished Corps had upon all occasions acted, and thanked them for their present loyal and patriotic offer. The Carnarvonshires were under orders for Ireland during the Rebellion, and again tendered their services in 1807, and were the first that landed in that country since the passing of the Act for the interchange of Militia. Since their arrival they have been formed into a Rifle Corps, the Arms, etc., supplied by the Government, and their Uniform changed from Scarlet to Green."

In announcing this change of role and uniform, *The Cambrian* was somewhat premature as the actual change did not take place until 1812.

The Records of the 4th Battalion, Royal Welch Fusiliers contain a copy of a letter which gave authority for the conversion.

"To Viscount Bulkeley,
Lord Lieutenant of Carnarvon,
My Lord,

Having submitted for the consideration of the Commander in Chief your Lordship's Letter of the 6th inst. with its enclosures, His Royal Highness being of the opinion that it would be advisable to form the Carnarvonshire Militia into a Rifle Corps, I have submitted to the Prince Regent your Lordship's proposal to that effect, and I have the satisfaction of acquainting you that His Royal Highness in the name and on behalf of His Majesty was graciously pleased to approve thereof.

I have the honour to be,
etc, etc,
Thomas Ryder."

Of interest also are the replies received to the offer of service in Spain and Portugal which had obviously been repeated in 1812.

"Whitehall, 1st December, 1812,

"To Viscount Bulkeley,
My Lord,

I have laid before the Prince Regent your Lordship's Letter of December 21st transmitting an offer from the Carnarvon Militia to serve in Spain and Portugal, and I am to acquaint your Lordship that His Royal Highness entertains the highest sense of this additional proof of the zeal and spirit which have uniformly been manifested by that diligent Corps,

I have the honour to be,
etc, etc,
Sidmouth."

and also

Horse Guards, 2nd December, 1812.

To Colonel Edwards,
commanding Royal Carnarvon Militia at Longford
Sir,

I have not failed to lay before the Commander in Chief your Letter of the 26th with its enclosures, and I am directed to acquaint you in reply, that if ever Government shall deem it expedient to adopt a measure accepting the service of Militia in the Peninsula, His Royal Highness will bear in mind the distinguished zeal manifested.

I have the honour to be,
etc, etc,
Sidmouth."

Whilst stationed in Longford and District the Corps was employed assisting the Revenue and Civil Power and in the protection of Military Stores.

The situation in Ireland in those early years of the 19th Century was in many ways similar to that which existed in that country in the 20's and in Ulster of the present day. At that time the fires of the Rebellion which had been put down in 1798 still smouldered; the Military were unpopular and acts of sabotage and terrorism were commonplace. In one such incident which took place in January 1813, a member of the Carnarvon Corps was seriously wounded. Reporting the matter on February 9th, *The Cambrian* had this to say — "On Saturday, January 9th, about the hour of three o'clock, two Sentinels in the Royal Carnarvonshire Rifle Corps, Guard at the Commisserat Stores in the town of Longford, Ireland, were maliciously fired upon by some person or persons unknown, and one of them was dangerously wounded. A liberal Subscription was immediately opened for the detection of the perpetrators of the diabolical act, amounting to upwards of £600, which we hope will have the desired effect of bringing the miscreants to condign punishment. Colonel Edwards and his Brother Officers have liberally subscribed £100." A noble and public spirited gesture no doubt, but one wonders what the unfortunate sentry got out of it other than his wound.

On the 21st March, 1813, a number of Men from the Corps volunteered their services into the Line, and a few days later, the 26th, the Regiment marched to Belfast. There they were stationed until May, and then shipped back to a convenient Port in mainland Britain from whence they marched to take up duties at Haddington Barracks, a few miles East of Edinburgh. In July the Corps took up duties at Berwick, but returned to Haddington in September. There, once again, the keeness of both Officers and Men to proceed on active service together, saw the whole volunteer for such duty with The Royal Scots (1st Foot). Events on the Continent were to prevent such a step, for Wellington's Victory at Toulouse on the 10th April had broken the French and brought about Napoleon's abdication. After years of War, the talk now turned to peace.

The Carnarvonshire Corps remained at Haddington until May 1814, at which time, its wartime duties completed, it was ordered home. On the 2nd June, the Corps broke its march at Liverpool for rest, and shortly thereafter was once again back in its native County.

On the 24th June its return was noted in *The Cambrian* — "The Anglesey, Flint, Carnarvon and Montgomery Regiments of Militia arrived in their native Counties last week, where they were received with loud and reiterated cheers after their long and arduous service."

A Royal Warrant dated 6th June, ordered the disembodiment of the Regiment and that took place at Caernarfon on Friday, 7th July, on completion of over eleven years of continuous service. A Note in the Records of the 4th R.W.F. gives 24th June, 1814, as the date of disembodiment, some twelve days earlier than the date given in *The Cambrian*. The 24th June ties in with the date of the disembodiment of the Mongomeryshire Militia, and in consequence may well be correct. ***The Cambrian*** in a later report once again gives 7th July, and also states "The Carnarvonshire Militia disembodied at Carnarvon on Friday se-night, previous to which they were entertained to a hot supper and plenty of 'Cwrw Da' by their respected Colonel, Richard Edwards, Esq., of Nanhoron."

1815-1854

The Militia of Caernarfonshire were not embodied due to the crisis of the 100 days, but were left dormant until 1820. In that year the Corps assembled in the County Town on the 15th May for 28 days training. The following year the Regiment assembled for 21 days on the 19th May, after which, with interest in Militia on the wane, they were left untrained until 1825. The Corps next assembled in 1831, in which year the Ballot was again enforced due to the amount of civil unrest in the country. In 1838, Richard Edwards retired after many long years of service and was succeeded as Commanding Officer by Major O.J.C. Nanney, late of the East India Company Service. In 1852 a resurgence of interest in the Militia took place which saw the Permanent Staff increased. In that year also Major Nanney was succeeded in the command by the Hon. Edward Gordon Douglas Pennant, late the Grenadier Guards, and whose family were closely connected with the County Slate Industry.

The revival of Militia in Caernarvonshire was brought about by the following letter:

"30th September, 1852,

By War Office Authority of that date, the Officer Commanding the Royal Carnarvon Rifle Regiment of Militia is authorised to raise as many men in the County of Carnarvon as are, or shall be wanting to complete the Companies of the Regiment to the number allowed on the Establishment."

The Establishment of the Corps at that date being:

Lieut. Colonel	— 1
Major	— 1
Captains	— 4
Lieutenants	— 4
Ensigns	— 4
Adjutant	— 1
Surgeon	— 1
Sergeant Major	— 1
Sergeants	— 13
Corporals	— 13
Drummers	— 3
Privates	— 388

Training in 1852 was held at Bangor as also the assemblies for 1853 and 1854.

1855-56

The Regiment was not, as in the case of some Welsh Militia Regiments, drawn out for Garrison Duty during the period of the War in the Crimea. It assembled for training at Caernarfon for a period slightly longer than the normal, and in consequence the Annual Training for 1856 was suspended. By far the most important development was the opening of a new stone Barracks near the town. Rated as Barracks in 1855 its two acres were occupied by three Offices, an Armoury, Magazine, eight Married Quarters, a Morris Tube Range, Drill Ground, Drill Shed, Band Room, Guard Room, two Cells, a Sergeants' Mess, six Storerooms and large gardens, which Establishment was then occupied by the Permanent Staff of the Corps.

1857-59

Annual Training took place at Caernarfon in September 1857, August 1858, and also in 1859, during which year a supply of the new pattern 1853 Enfield Rifles was delivered to the Corps.

1860

A War Office Letter dated 28th July directed that the Militia of the Counties of Anglesey and Caernarfonshire be united:

"H.M. Vice Lieutenant in the County of Carnarvon,

Sir,

With reference to the correspondence that as taken place relative to the amalgamation of the Militia Regiments of the Counties of Carnarvon and Anglesey, I have now the honour to inform you that with a view of the convenience of the Service, Her Majesty has been graciously pleased to direct that these two Counties shall unite in forming one Battalion of Militia, instead of two separate Battalions, and that its Establishment shall consist as follows, and that it shall be designated The Royal Carnarvon and Anglesey Rifles Militia.

1 Lieutenant Colonel
1 Major
8 Captains
8 Lieutenants
8 Ensigns
1 Adjutant
1 Quartermaster
1 Surgeon
1 Assistant Surgeon
1 Sergeant Major
1 Quartermaster Sergeant
1 Sergeant Instructor (Musketry)
1 Bugle Major

1 Orderly Room Clerk
1 Paymaster Sergeant
1 Hospital Sergeant
22 Sergeants
22 Corporals
8 Buglers
644 Privates

1861-1866

In May 1861, the 1853 Enfield Rifles were withdrawn, the Carnarvonshire quota receiving in their place 417 of the Short Pattern complete with Rammers, Bayonets, Scabbards, Stoppers and Snap Caps.

The venue for Annual Training between 1860 and 1866 was Caernarfon, the Regiment assembling in the following Months:

1860, 1861	— September
1862	— May
1863, 1864	— April
1865	— May
1866	— April

1867

On the 11th March, 1867, a Letter was received authorising the separation of the Carnarvon Militia from that of Anglesey, and giving the Establishment for the reorganised regiment.

1 Lieut. Colonel
1 Major
4 Captains
4 Lieutenants
4 Ensigns
1 Adjutant
1 Quartermaster
1 Surgeon
1 Assistant Surgeon
1 Sergeant Major
1 Quartermaster Sergeant
1 Sergeant Instructor (Musketry)
1 Orderly Room Clerk
1 Bugle Major
1 Hospital Sergeant
10 Permanent Staff Sergeants
4 Volunteer Sergeants (i.e. Militia as opposed to Permanent Staff)
14 Corporals
4 Drummers/Buglers
388 Privates

Annual Training took place in April during which the Corps was inspected by Colonel J.C.H. Jones, Commanding 14th Depot Battalion. In his Report he requested that the Commanding Officer make it known to the Regiment that he was perfectly satisfied with the regiment in every respect and that it would be his duty to make a most favourable comment upon its state of efficiency.

The year also saw the Sergeants of the Permanent Staff of the Corps armed with the Snider Breech Loading Rifle.

1868-1872

The Regiment assembled annually for training during the months stated:
1868 — April
1869 — May
1870, 71 and 72 — April, the venue in each case being Caernarfon.

1873

The Regiment assembled at Caernarfon in April, the following Officers being in attendance:
Colonel Lord Penrhyn
Lieut. Colonel J.H.V. Williams
Major Platt
Captain Cragg, Captain J. Wynn-Griffiths, Captain D.G. Griffiths, Captain H. Wayne, Captain W.K. Hayward, Captain E.H.B. Gladstone, Surgeon Richards also the Adjutant.

1874

During the 1874 Training, the Corps was inspected by Colonel Drysdale, Commanding 14th Depot Battalion. Eleven Men were enrolled in the Militia Reserve during the period.

A Letter dated 8th May gave Royal approval to augment the Establishment of the Regiment by two Companies.

1875

The Regiment assembled at Caernarfon in April, 560 strong, and was inspected by Colonel Cooper, Commanding 23rd Brigade, on the 7th May. Prior to the main assembly, 225 Recruits had attended Preliminary Training.

1876-1877

The Regiment trained during both years at Caernarfon, 816 being present for the 1877 training.

1878

The Regiment assembled at Caernarfon in April. On the 4th of that month instructions were received for the mobilisation of the Militia Reserve, which task was to be effected on the 19th. Of 205 Men of the Royal Carnarvon Militia Reserve, 195 reported for Army Service, a number of which were immediately sent to join the 1st Battalion, 23rd Foot, Royal Welsh Fusiliers at Iniskilling, Ireland. A second draft was sent to the same destination on the 29th April. Of the Reservists who reported for duty, 25 were found unfit to proceed on Medical grounds.

1879-1880

The Regiment trained at Caernarfon, assembling at the Barracks in April. The procedure was repeated in 1880.

1881

The Regiment assembled at the Caernarfon Barracks in April to train for the last time under the proud old title of Royal Carnarvon Rifles. On the 1st July, in accordance with instructions given in General Order No.41/1881 dated 1st May, the Royal Carnarvon Militia was redesignated as the 4th (Militia) Battalion, Royal Welsh Fusiliers. The year saw 194 Recruits trained as Militiamen, and of the numbers present at Annual Training, 484 were born in the County, 301 originated from other Welsh Counties, 20 came from Scotland and 56 were Irishmen.

1882

The Regiment assembled at Caernarfon in April. During the training it was inspected in Review Order on the 16th May by Major General W.G. Cameron, C.B., commanding Northern District, and on the 18th May, in Marching Order by Colonel, Hon. C. Mostyn, C.B., commanding 23rd Regimental District.

1883

The Regiment assembled for training on the 7th May, and was inspected by Colonel Hon. Savage Mostyn, C.B., on the 30th.

179 Recruits received Preliminary Drill in addition to the annual training, 395 of the Men present were born in the County, 341 originated in England or other Welsh Counties, 40 were Irishmen and 3 were Scots.

1884-1886

Training took place at Caernarfon each year for the period stated. In 1885 the Regiment assembled on March 2nd, and were complimented by Major General W.A. Willis, C.B, commanding Northern District for appearance and drill.

On the 21st May, at the ceremony held at Cae Toplis near the town the Battalion received new Colours from the hands of Mrs Platt, wife of the Colonel. The occasion saw a very large gathering of interested spectators, the ground being kept by the Carnarvon Battery, Royal Naval Artillery Volunteers commanded by Lieut. C.A. Jones.

Mrs Platt in handing over the Colours to Lieutenants Lecknam and Hamilton, the two senior Subalterns of the Battalion, said "Colonel Platt, Commissioned Officers, Non Commissioned Officers and Men, I feel deeply the honour you have done me in requesting me to present these beautiful Colours today. I do so with the greatest pleasure, feeling sure that you will always regard them with the love and veneration which they so well deserve, and when occasion demands, you will rally around them as the representatives of the honour of your Queen."

The 1886 training commenced on the 8th March with Preliminary Drill for 204 Recruits. Of the numbers present at the main training period, 369 were Caernarfonshire Men, 130 originated in England or other Welsh Counties, 83 were Irishmen and 8 were Scots.

1887

Annual Training took place in June, the Battalion being housed under canvas at Cae Toplis Field. On the 21st of that month the unit paraded and fired a Feu de Joie in honour of the Jubilee of Her Majesty Queen Victoria. Other units present at this public occasion were the 3rd Volunteer Battalion, Royal Welsh Fusiliers commanded by Captain Charles Rees, the Caernarfon Battery of the 1st Cheshire and Carnarvonshire Artillery Volunteers, commanded by Captain Turner, the Caernarfon Royal Naval Reserve detachment commanded by Chief Officer W. Bailey, and the Royal Naval Reserve Volunteers commanded by Lieut. Charles Jones.

1888-1889

In 1888 the Battalion assembled on the 26th March for training, and in 1889 on the 3rd June. The venue on both occasions was a tented camp at Cae Toplis Field. In the latter year the Inspecting Officer made the following remarks concerning the Men.

Of good physique, well drilled, but with a poor standard of Musketry. He also stated that their conduct during training was not as good as it ought to have been.

The observations of the Recruiting Officer for the Army and Militia in the Caernarfonshire Recruiting District for 1889 are of some interest, and were based on four months experience in those parts.

1. The gross ignorance of the greater part of the population, more especially in the agricultural districts, on all subjects connected to the Army, such as the Social status of a Soldier, his prospects, terms of service, etc, was a great obstacle to recruiting.
2. The absolute necessity of having Welsh speaking Sergeants on the Permanent Staff of the Battalion in order to guarantee some success.
3. The mischief wrought by discharged Bad Characters who decry the Army life.
4. The want of patriotism in small Employers of Labour who refuse to employ Militia and Reserve Men.

He also pointed out the hardship suffered by detached Recruiting Sergeants in such a poor recruiting district, for no matter how hard he worked, he was never able to draw in sufficient Recruits to recoup himself, and so suffered a financial loss.

His suggestions for remedying the Recruiting situation are equally interesting.

1. That a body of Troops should be encamped in the District and move about in it.

If possible, this should be their own Regiment. This would put the people in touch with Soldiers and allow them to see for themselves that the Army was a respectable profession where the Men were cared for.

2. The better advertising of the Service at Post Offices and Police Stations.

3. The Officers Commanding the 1st and 2nd Battalions, Royal Welsh Fusiliers, should be instructed to send in Welsh speaking Sergeants to fill the vacancies on the Recruiting and Militia Staff, setting aside if necessary, the ten year service requirement laid down in Queen's Regulations.

As will be seen, his voice and opinion did not go unheard.

1890

The Battalion assembled at Caernarfon on the 24th March and trained for 56 days. The annual Inspection was carried out by Colonel R.S. Liddell, commanding 23rd Regimental District, and the Men dismissed to their homes on the 14th June.

1891

The 1891 training saw the Battalion move away from Caernarfon for the first time for that purpose, the venue being Altcar Camp, near Liverpool. Colonel R.S. Liddell in his Inspection Report stated that he was well satisfied with the behaviour of the Men throughout the training, especially taking into account that it was the first time the unit had trained away from Caernarfon. He described the Men as Soldierlike, Clean and creditably drilled, and added that due attention had been paid to their proficiency at Musketry.

On completion of training in mid June, the Battalion was conveyed back to Caernarfon, and having returned their Arms and military Kit, the Men were dismissed to their homes.

1892-1893

In 1892 the Battalion assembled on March 21st and in 1893 on the 29th May, the venue being Cae Toplis Camp, Caernarfon, and the duration 27 days. In 1893 the Men were grouped under a new system of Local Companies in an effort to stimulate recruitment and the competitive spirit. Under the system Men were posted if possible to the Company of the District to which they belonged, and again, where possible, a Captain from that District was given command of the Company. The new Company designations were as follows:

Old Title	Local Title	Officer Commanding
'A' Coy	Porthmadog Coy	Captain J.R. Owen
'B' Coy	Conway Coy	Major Hon. H.R. Lloyd Mostyn

'C' Coy	Caernarfon Coy	Major Turner (Plas Brereton)
'D' Coy	Lleyn Coy	Captain Theobald
'E' Coy	Bala Coy	Captain W. Buckley
'F' Coy	Dolgelley Coy	Captain R.Ll. Richards (Caerynwch)
'D' Coy	Ffestiniog Coy (Merioneth Quarries)	Captain H. Price
'H' Coy	Bangor Coy	Captain H. Jones Williams

In this year it was noted that the shooting of the Battalion was greatly improved, the most proficient Company being that of Caernarfon. The Best Shot in the Battalion was Private Steven Grayham of the Dolgellau Company — understandable, taking into account that he was an ex-regular soldier of 12 years service.

Best Shot for the Caernarfonshire Companies was Private Owen Edwards of Porthmadog, and winner of the Lord Lieutenant's Prize for Merioneth was Private Griffith Pierce from Ffestiniog.

Best Shot amongst Recruits that year was Private Owen Lewis of the Caernarfon Company.

As has been previously stated Recruiters in the District drew in Men for both the Regular Army and the Militia, and if surnames of the N.C.O.'s are anything to go by, it is doubtful if many of them were Welsh speaking.

Colour Sgt Higgins
Brynkir, Chwilog, Cricieth, Dolbenmaen, Porthmadog, Tremadog, Penmorfa and Beddgelert.
Colour Sgt Oakley
Penmaenmawr, Conway, Llandudno, Colwyn Bay, Llanrwst, Trefriw, Bettws y Coed.
Colour Sgt Boundy
Caernarvon, Porthdinorwig and District.
Sergeant Instructor Moore
Cwmyglo, Ebenezer, Llanberis, Dinas, Llanwnda, Groeslon, Llandwrog.
Colour Sgt Flaherty
Penygroes, Llanllyfni, Pwllheli, Four Crosses, Sarn, Abersoch.
Sergeant Roberts
Bala, Llandderfel, Corwen, Frongoch.
Colour Sgt Pemberton
Sarnau, Harlech, Barmouth, Arthog, Penmaenpool, Dolgellau, Llanelltyd, Tynygroes, Llanfachreth, Bontnewydd, Drwsynant, Trawsfynydd.
Sergeant Morris
Llwyngwril, Towyn, Llanegryn, Abergynolwyn, Aberdyfi, Corris, Dinas Mawddwy.

Colour Sgt Cush
Pontypant, Dolwyddelen, Roman Bridge, Blaenau Ffestiniog, Tan y Bwlch, Maentwrog, Penrhyndeudraeth.
Sergeant Coombes
Bangor, Bethesda, Llanfairfechan, Aber, Menai Bridge.
Sergeant Lancets
Bodorgan, Ty'n y Groes, Valley, Llanerchymedd, Llangefni, Amlwch, Cemmaes.
Sergeant Day
Holyhead, Aberffraw, Malltraeth, Newborough, Brynsiencyn, Llanfair P.G., Menai Bridge.
Sergeant Marshall
Caernarfon Town.

The Recruiters responsible for Anglesey districts also recruited for the Royal Anglesey Engineers Militia.

1894

Prior to the 1894 training the following Recruiting Poster was distributed throughout the Battalion Recruiting District, and its tone shows that the action called for by the District Recruiting Officer in 1889 had not gone entirely unheeded.

CARNARVON AND MERIONETH MILITIA

SOME MORE WELSHMEN ARE WANTED FOR THE MILITIA TRAINING THIS YEAR AT DOLGELLEY ON THE 21st MAY FOR 27 DAYS.

RECRUITS DRILL AT CARNARFON ON THE 19th MARCH FOR 63 DAYS.

GOOD PAY, GOOD FOOD, GOOD CLOTHES, BOUNTY FROM £1 to £2.10.0.

EACH MAN GETS A FLANNEL SHIRT, A PAIR OF BOOTS, AND 2 PAIRS OF SOCKS FOR HIMSELF AT THE END OF THE TRAINING.

APPLY TO THE POLICE, OR TO THE LOCAL RECRUITER, OR TO THE RECRUITING OFFICER AT THE BARRACKS CARNARVON.

IN THIS MILITIA, WELSHMEN GET EVERY HELP. THEY ARE DRILLED BY WELSH SERGEANTS UNDER A WELSH ADJUTANT.

NONE BUT REAL WELSHMEN NEED APPLY.

J. GRIFFITH,
CAPTAIN, ROYAL WELSH FUSILIERS,
RECRUITING OFFICER,
CARNARFON, 6th MARCH, 1894.

Later that year, the Battalion having first assembled at Caernarfon proceeded by rail to Dolgellau where they were housed under canvas on the Marian. There they were inspected by Colonel C.W. Wilson, commanding 23rd Regimental District, on the 14th June.

1895-1896

Caernarfon was the venue for the 1895 training, the old hands assembling on the 27th May on completion of the Recruits Preliminary Drill. In 1896 the Battalion paid its second visit to Dolgellau, assembling at Caernarfon on the 18th May for 27 days. Prior to its return to Caernarfon on June 13th, Colonel Platt received the following letter from the Dolgellau Urban District Council.

"The Mayor, Mr J. Meyrick, proposed, and it was unanimously resolved, that the Council gladly welcome back to Dolgelley, the Officers and Men of the 4th Battalion, Royal Welsh Fusiliers for their Annual Training, and hope to have the pleasure of welcoming them on many future occasions.

Signed: Elliot Davies,
Clerk,
to Dolgelley Urban District Council."

1897

Preliminary Drill for Recruits commenced at Caernarfon on the 15th March, the full Battalion assembling at the same place for 27 days on May 17th.

The year also saw the re-equipping of the Battalion with the improved white buff leather Valise Equipment 1882 Pattern.

1898

Cae Toplis Camp, Carnarvon, was the venue for the 1898 training. Recruits assembling on the 21st March, and the main body on the 23rd May for 27 days. Musketry Training was carried out at Llanberis to which place each Company marched in turn, a round trip of some seventeen and a half miles.

In June, the Battalion was inspected in Castle Square, Caernarfon, by the Field Marshall, Commanding in Chief, The Right Hon. G.G. Viscount Wolseley K.P., G.C.B., C.M.G.

Present at the training were 20 Officers and 544 Other Ranks. 20 Officers and 46 Other Ranks were absent for various reasons.

1899

On the 25th April, the Battalion provided a Guard of Honour at Caernarfon on the occasion of the visit of the Duke and Duchess of York to the town. Annual Training commenced on the 29th May, the unit proceeding to Dolgellau, Merionethshire, by rail where they were encamped on the Llwyn Field near the town. Returning to Caernarfon on completion the Men were dismissed to their homes on the 24th June, 1899.

The outbreak of the Boer War in October, and the failure of the War Office to embody the Battalion prompted the Commanding Officer to write the following letter:

24th November, 1899,

To, The Officer Commanding,
23rd Regimental District,
Wrexham.
Sir,

I learn with much regret that the 4th Battalion, Royal Welsh Fusiliers is not amongst the Militia Battalions embodied. I believe that the 3rd Battalion, Royal Welsh Fusiliers has been embodied on a former occasion, and was also selected for the Guard of Honour on the occasion of Her Majesty's Jubilee.

It is very discouraging to the Officers and Men of the 4th Battalion to be again passed over.

I beg to point out, that up to last year, when recruiting in South Wales was specially sanctioned, the Battalion was for many years numerically much stronger.

I herewith submit that if it is the intention of Government to call out the Militia for six months, the 4th Battalion may be embodied for the latter half of that period to relieve the 3rd Battalion.

I have the honour to be, Sir,
Your Obedient Servant,
Llewelyn J. Evans,
Lieut. Colonel, commanding, 4th Bn, Royal Welsh Fusiliers."

1900

On the 1st March, 1900, an Order was received for the formation of a Draft from the Militia Reserve of the Battalion.

Fifty-three Men were promptly called up, clothed and equipped at the Barracks, Caernarfon, and having been certified medically fit, left to join the details of the Royal Welsh Fusiliers stationed at Crownhill Barracks, Plymouth.

On the day of their departure, the townspeople of Caernarfon turned out en masse and gave them an enthusiastic send off along the route and at the station.

Later, a party, with 15 Men of the 3rd Battalion sailed for South Africa on the S.S. Gaka under the command of Lieut. Colonel Holroyd. On arrival at the Cape, the draft proceeded by rail to Kimberley where they replaced casualties in the 1st Battalion suffered during the Tugela/Ladysmith operations.

A few weeks after their arrival they were in action at Rooidam and involved in the march to the Relief of Mafeking.

Back home, Recruit training commenced on the 19th March, and an Order of Embodiment was received for the Battalion. An Advance Party was sent on ahead to Devonport to take over a section of Crownhill Barracks. On the

W.O., STAFF-SERGTS. & SERGTS. 3rd BATTALION ROYAL WELSH FUSILIERS,
Crownhill Barracks, near Plymouth. October 1900

3rd Batt. Royal Welsh Fusiliers' Mascot.

11th May, the whole Battalion was assembled under the command of Colonel Evans, proceeded to Plymouth that same day by two Special Trains. The total number of All Ranks joining, was 562.

On the 22nd May a Draft of 40 Militia Reservists proceeded from Devonport to Bulford to join details of the Royal Welsh Fusiliers forming up in a draft to join the 1st Battalion in South Africa, and on the 21st June were followed by another 50 who joined details of the Devon Regiment waiting to proceed to join the 1st and 2nd Devons at the seat of War.

The last draft provided by the Battalion left for Bulford on the 13th of July and were destined to join the 1st R.W.F. at the Cape. Reports filtering back from South Africa spoke highly of those Men, the Commanding Officer of the 1st R.W.F. commenting favourable on the stamina and marching prowess of all the Militia drafts.

Meanwhile at home, the Battalion carried out Garrison Duty in Plymouth and District and also took part in a Brigade Camp at Yenadon Down, Dartmoor, between the 17th and 22nd September.

On the 12th October, the Battalion was inspected at Crownhill by Colonel Walford, R.A., Acting General Officer commanding Western District. Its Garrison Duty ended on the 16th October when the Officers and Men entrained for Caernarfon. On arrival the following day, the Battalion formed up in Castle Square and was inspected by Colonel R.B. Mainwaring, C.M.G., Officer Commanding 23rd Regimental District. In his remarks to the troops, he commented favourably on their appearance, and particularly on the good quality of their conduct during the embodiment. The Battalion then returned to the Barracks, where having turned in their Arms and Equipment, the Men were dismissed to their homes.

1901

In view of the recent embodiment, only the Recruits assembled for training in 1901.

1902

In 1902 the Battalion continued with its efforts to take account of the high number of potential, but Welsh speaking, recruits in its catchment area. At the Barracks, Carnarvon, there were several Welsh speaking Sergeants on the Staff, and much of the preliminary instruction was given to recruits in their own language. It was noted that there was deep-rooted objection to having Drill Sergeants who spoke English only, and it was estimated that the Battalion had lost at least 50 recruits for that reason.

On the 9th May, the Battalion provided a Guard of Honour of 3 Officers, and 100 Other Ranks who paraded with the Colours and Band at the Palace, Bangor, on the occasion of the visit of the Prince and Princess of Wales to the Cathedral City. On the 19th May, the Battalion entrained for Altcar, near

Liverpool, for annual training, returning to Caernarfon for dismissal on the 29th June. Present at training were 11 Officers and 442 Other Ranks.

1903

Preliminary Drill commenced at the Barracks, Carnarvon, on April 6th, the main body assembling on June 8th and thence proceeding to Parkhouse Camp, Salisbury Plain, for 27 days training. There the Goat, gift of His Majesty to the Battalion, died. An application for a replacement from the Royal Herd at Windsor was sent off immediately.

1904

The Battalion trained at Altcar for 27 days commencing 6th June. There, in company with 3. R.W.F., it formed the Royal Welsh Fusilier Militia Brigade commanded by Brigadier General R.B. Mainwaring, C.M.G. 15 Officers, 393 Other Ranks attended. The Battalion received a good inspection report, but was warned to pay more attention to recruit training if standards were to be properly maintained.

1905

Assembling on May 15th, the Battalion proceeded by train to camp under canvas at Conway, where once again they were brigaded with 3. R.W.F. The inhabitants of Conway enjoyed the military presence, and showed both curiosity and appreciation by visiting the Camp and attending the Band Concerts in large numbers. In attendance also, was the Regimental Goat, His Majesty's kind replacement for the Goat who had passed on in 1903. Sadly, this Goat also died, and on this occasion, no replacement was available from the Royal Herd due to reduced numbers. The situation was saved by Lady Augusta Mostyn, who presented the Battalion with a somewhat rougher but undoubtedly hardier Welsh replacement. This animal survived and remained fully active for what remained of the lifespan of the Battalion.

1906

Preliminary Drill for recruits commenced at Caernarfon on the 4th April — a period of training supervised entirely by Welsh speaking staff. Assembling on the 4th June, the Battalion again entrained for Conway, where as in the previous year, the Militiamen were made more than welcome.

1907

Conway was again the venue for Battalion annual training. This was to be 4. R.W.F.'s last annual Camp. On the 24th December, a Special Army Order was received which gave details of a scheme for the provision, organisation and training of a Special Reserve. Existing Infantry Militia Ballations were to be reduced from 124 to 101, and amongst those earmarked for disbandment was 4. R.W.F., lineal successor of the old Carnarvonshire County Militia. Petitions from both Battalion and residents of the County proved unsuccessful, and so preparations were put in hand for the final stand down of an old established and respected Corps.

1908

The 4th Battalion, Royal Welsh Fusiliers, ceased to exist on March 31st, 1908, and thus brought to a close 146 years of County Militia history.

Footnotes

1. Article.
   The Society and Garrison of Fort Williamsburg.
   E.A. Jones, F.S.A. Y Cymmrodor. Vol XLIV. 1935
2. E.A. Jones, F.S.A.
3. As for 1.
4. Popular Protests in Wales, 1793-1835
5. North Wales Gazette

Other Sources

The Cambrian

LIST OF OFFICERS

1779

Captain Commandant, Lieut. Colonel, The Lord Newborough
Lieut. John Holland
Ensign Ellis Wynne
Adjutant Hugh Lloyd
Quartermaster Jenkin Owen
Surgeon Thomas Davies

1781

Colonel Lord Newborough	2.8.1780
Captain William Williams	2.8.1780
Lieut. David Evans	14.9.1780
Ensign John Lloyd Thomas	2.8.1780
Ensign James Fitzgibbons	18.1.1871
Quartermaster Jenkin Owen	20.4.1778
Surgeon Richard Thompson	24.10.1780

Agent: John Fenwick — Westminster

1782

Major Ellis Wynne	June 1781
Captain Thomas Williams	2.8.1781
Lieut. David Evans	14.9.1780
Lieut. Lancelot Hilton	20.10.1781
Ensign J. Lloyd Thomas	2.8.1780
Ensign James Fitzgibbon	18.1.1871 (also Adjutant)

1793

Captain Commandant Richard Edwards	13.5.1793
Lieut. John Jones	13.4.1793
Ensign Richard Poole	6.8.1793

Jones also held the appointments of Adjutant and Quartermaster whilst Poole was also Surgeon to the Corps.
The List for 1796 is similar but with the following additions

Captain Evan Pritchard	6.8.1795
Lieut. Richard Jones	3.3.1795

and with also Richard Edwards promoted Major Commandant with effect from 24th April, 1795.

1800

Lieut. Colonel Commandant Richard Edwards	12.6.1798
Captain Griffith Griffith	10.3. 1798
Lieut. Richard Jones	3.3.1795
Lieut. John Lloyd Jones	15.5.1799
Lieut. John Taylor	27.8.1799
Ensign Richard Poole	1.8.1793
Ensign William Jones	14.10.1799
Adjutant Richard Jones	28.9.1796
Quartermaster Richard Jones	2.6.1797

No Surgeon listed.
Regimental Agent was Mr John Fenwick, Mill Bank St., Westminster.

1803 (July)

Major Commandant, Lieut. Colonel Richard Edwards of Nanhoron	24.4.1795
Captain J.H. Hampton of Henllys, Anglesea	15.3.1801
Lieut. William Jones of Werglodd Fawr	15.6.1800
Ensign John James	1.9.1801
Lieut. and Adjutant Richard Jones	1.3.1800

Agent: Mr Gilpin, The Strand.

1804 (December)

Colonel Richard Edwards
Major J. Hampton Hampton
Captain D. Griffith
Lieut. W. Jones
Ensign G. Watkins
Surgeon E. Carreg
Paymaster W. Jones
Adjutant S. Ellis

1808 (April)

Colonel Richard Edwards	21.2.1804
Major J.H. Hampton	29.7.1803
Captain Richard Jones	9.11.1807
1st Lieut. William Jones	15.6.1800
2nd Lieut. Samuel Prytherch	25.6.1807
Lieut. and Adjutant Stephen Ellis	
Surgeon Edward Carrey (or Carreg)	
Paymaster William Jones	

1814 (August)

Major Commandant, Colonel Richard Evans	25.2.1804
Captain Richard Jones	9.11.1807
1st Lieut. T. Churchill	25.9.1808
1st Lieut. Hugh Hughes	12.1.1814
Captain and Adjutant J.T. Sewell	20.12.1811
Surgeon E. Carreg	23.7.1803

1816 (June)

Major Commandant, Colonel Richard Evans	21.2.1804
Captain Richard Jones	9.11.1807
1st Lieut. Thomas Churchill	25.9.1803 (also Paymaster)
1st Lieut. Hugh Hughes	12.1.1814
Capt. and Adjutant James Thomas Sewell	20.12.1811
Surgeon Edward Carreg	23.7.1803
Agent: Bruce, 47 Parliament St.	

1820 (September)

No change except for the addition of	
2nd Lieut. William Roberts	2.5.1820

1825 (September)

Major Commandant Richard Edwards	21.2.1804
Captain Samuel Owen Priestly	23.5.1825
1st Lieut. Thomas Churchill	25.9.1808 (also Paymaster)
1st Lieut. Hugh Hughes	12.1.1814
2nd Lieut. William Jones	19.5.1825
2nd Lieut. Henry Turner	23.5.1825
Captain and Adjutant James Thomas Sewell	20.12.1811
Surgeon Edward Carreg	23.7.1803

1852

Colonel, The Hon. E.G.D. Pennant	30.8.1852
Captain C. Griffith Wynne, D.L., J.P.	8.10.1852
Captain R.W.J. Bulkeley	18.10.1852
Captain J.V.H. Williams, D.L., J.P.	4.11.1852
Captain William Griffith Griffith	4.11.1852
Lieut. T.E.L. Hunt	20.10.1852
Lieut. J. Rowland	201.10.1852
Lieut. T.W.W. Jones	20.10.1852
Lieut. A. Wyatt	20.10.1852
Lieut. W. Wynn	26.11.1852
Ensign F.M. Allen	26.10.1852
Ensign J.B. Williams	20.10.1852

Captain and Adjutant P.A. Iremonger (late 56th Regt)	22.10.1852
Surgeon J. Richards	26.11.1852

1854 (Harts)

Lieut. Colonel Commandant Hon. E.G.D. Pennant (late Gren. Guards)	30.8.1852
Major John McDonald	
Captain C. Griffith Wynne, D.L., J.P.	18.10.1852
Captain J.V.H. Williams, D.L., J.P.	4.11.1852
Captain Wm Griffith Griffith	4.11.1852
Captain John Rowlands	19.5.1853
Lieut. Thomas Edward Lloyd Hunt	20.10.1852
Lieut. Arthur Wyatt	20.10.1852
Lieut. William Wynne	26.11.1852
2nd Lieut. T.W.W. Jones	20.10.1852
2nd Lieut. F.M. Allen	20.10.1852
2nd Lieut. J.B. Williams	20.10.1852
Captain and Adjutant P.A. Iremonger	22.10.1852
Surgeon John Richards	26.11.1852

1861 (Harts)

Hon. Colonel Hon. E.G. Douglas Pennant	24.8.1858
Lieut. Colonel John McDonald, D.L.	24.12.1858
Major John Vincent Hawkesley Williams	25.8. 1858
Captain John Bailey Williams	24.12.1858
Captain Owen Massey Jones	30.7.1859
Captain Charles Abbott Delmar (late 9th Dragoons)	4.9.1859
Captain Griffith H. Owen	28.11.1860
Lieut. Henry Kneeshaw	29.9.1860
Ensign Henry Rumsey Williams	7.5.1860
Ensign John Poole	7.5.1860
Captain and Adjutant Edward D. Nares (late 9th Regt)	20.7.1859
Surgeon John Richards	26.11.1852
Agents: Messrs Cox & Co.	

1863 (March)

Hon. Colonel Hon. E.G. Douglas Pennant	24.8.1858
Lieut. Colonel John McDonald	24.12.1858
otherwise similar to 1861 except for the addition of	
Ensign Henry Platt	18.2.1863

1869 (November)

Hon. Colonel Lord Penrhyn	24.8.1858
Lieut. Colonel Hugh Jones (late 73rd Foot)	7.1.1865

Major J.V.H. Williams	25.8.1858
Captain Henry Kneeshaw	18.3.1865
Captain Henry Platt	11.5.1866
Captain Wallace Wm Cragg	1.5.1867
Captain J.G.W. Griffith (late 86th Foot)	6.7.1868
Lieut. D.G. Griffiths (late 3rd Foot)	14.7.1869
Captain and Adjutant Edw Deane Nares	20.7.1859
Surgeon John Richards	26.11.1852

1873 (April)

Hon. Colonel Lord Penrhyn	24.8.1858
Lieut. Colonel Commandant J.V.H. Williams	23.2.1872
Major Henry Platt	11.3.1872
Captain W.W. Cragg	1.5.1867
Captain J.G.W. Griffiths	16.7.1868
Captain D.G. Griffiths	9.8.1870
Captain H. Wayne	3.4.1871
Lieut. W.K. Hayward	3.4.1871
Lieut. F.R.C. Paget	6.4.1871
Lieut. C.H.B. Gladstone	6.5.1871
Captain and Adjutant E.D. Nares	15.6.1859
Surgeon J. Richards, M.D.	26.11.1852

1880 (November)

Hon. Colonel Lord Penrhyn	24.8.1858
Lieut. Colonel Commandant J.V.H. Williams	23.2.1872
Major H. Platt	11.3.1872
Major W.W. Cragg	2.12.1876
Captain J.G.W. Griffith	16.7.1868
Captain H. Wayne	3.4.1871
Captain W.K. Hayward	29.4.1874
Captain C. Morgan (late 23rd Regt)	10.10.1874
Captain J.C. Bradshaw (late 23rd Regt)	17.1.1877
Captain Ch.H.B. Gladstone	21.4.1877
Captain H.L. Peel	24.4.1880
Captain J.H. Platt	24.7.1880
Lieut. O.L.J. Evans	7.2.1877
Lieut. F.W. Turner	7.2.1877
Lieut. E.A. Mayhew	6.8.1879
Lieut. J.D. M.' Garel Hogg	13.9.1879
Lieut. H.R.H. Lloyd Mostyn	2.4.1880
Lieut. S. Platt	20.10.1880
Lieut. A.C.T. Orde Powlett	20.10.1880
2nd Lieut. H.A. Duff	10.12.1879

Captain and Adjutant G.C.E. Rowley (late 23rd Fus.)	28.8.1879
Quartermaster Wm Gray	31.8.1878
Med. Officer J. Richards, M.D.	26.11.1852

1885

Hon. Colonel Lord Penrhyn	24.8.1858
Lieut. Colonel H. Platt	22.10.1884
Major W.W. Cragg	2.12.1870
Major H. Wayne	13.12.1884
Captain C. Morgan	10.10.1874
Captain J.C. Bradshaw	17.1.1877
Captain H.L. Peel	24.4.1880
Captain O.L.J. Evans	25.4.1881
Captain F.W. Turner	14.3.1883
Captain Hon. H.R. Lloyd Mostyn	9.1.1884
Captain H.R. Jones Williams	7.1.1885
Captain A.D.S. Hamilton Douglas	20.6.1885
Lieut. B.T. Sockham	18.1.1882
Lieut. H.O. Morgan	20.5.1884
Lieut. A.N. Wyatt	7.1.1885
Lieut. W.L. Thursby	28.1.1885
Lieut. C.E.H. Poole	4.4.1885
Major and Adjutant S.B. Blythe (2/RWF)	1.9.1884
Quartermaster H.E. White	10.12.1884
M.O. J. Richards, M.D.	26.11.1852

1896 (December)

Hon. Colonel Lord Penrhyn	6.3.1895
Lieut. Colonel H. Platt	22.10.1884
Major O.L.J. Evans	25.4.1888
Major Hon. H.R.H. Lloyd Mostyn	14.11.1894
Captain G.R. Owen	28.3.1890
Captain A.H. Price	20.9.1890
Captain H.R. Jones Williams	7.1.1885
Captain R.E.L. Richards	21.11.1891
Captain W. Buckley	6.2.1892
Captain E.F.C. Evanson	10.2.1893
Captain A.R.P. McCartney Filgate	2.1.1893
Captain S. Reynolds	28.10.1896
Lieut. W.D. Jones	3.10.1891
Lieut. E.J.W. Platt	12.3.1892
Lieut. A.E. Lewis	8.4.1893
Lieut. C.P. Holroyd	3.3.1894
Lieut. W.E.S. Butson	2.1.1895

Lieut. F.H. Lloyd	18.5.1896
Lieut. Hon. C.R. Clegg-Hill	28.10.1896
2nd Lieut. F. Swetenham	6.3.1895
2nd Lieut. E.B. Jones	24.7.1895
2nd Lieut. C.C.H. Potter	27.11.1895
2nd Lieut. L.N. Williams	19.2.1896
2nd Lieut. S.P.W. Priestly	28.10.1896
Captain & Adjutant A.F. Cooper (RWF)	1.9.1894
Quartermaster H.E. White (Hon. Captain)	10.12.1884

1908 (February)

Hon. Colonel E.S. Lord Penrhyn	1.7.1907
Lieut. Colonel H.R.H. Lloyd Mostyn	13.5.1903
Major H.R. Jones Williams	13.6.1903
Captain A.H. Price	20.9.1890
Captain A.R.P. McCartney Filgate	2.1.1895
Captain C.P. Holroyd	13.5.1903
Captain E.B. Jones	20.5.1903
Captain J.H. Brennan	4.6.1903
Captain H.R. Maxted	22.11.1905
Lieut. F.G. Waddington	31.8.1900
Lieut. T.L. Pritchard	23.2.1901
Lieut. J. Ormrod	4.10.1902
Lieut. W.W. Kirkby	19.12.1903
2nd Lieut. Hon. R.C.L. Mostyn	11.11.1905
2nd Lieut. J. Colquhoun	18.2.1907
2nd Lieut. R.G. Braken	25.4.1907
Lieut. T.L. Pritchard (Inst. of Musketry)	
Captain & Adjutant Hon. C.R. Clegg Hill, D.S.O. (RWF)	1.9.1904
Q.M. and Hon. Captain R.S. Ransome	

OTHER OFFICERS KNOWN TO HAVE SERVED IN THE REGIMENT

Captain Hugh Jones of Caerhun (later assumed the surname Davies)	c.1864
Lieut. Hugh Williams of Plas Ponthir, Nr. Bangor	c.1864

OTHER OFFICERS KNOWN TO HAVE SERVED IN THE REGIMENT

Allen. Lieut. L.P.	25.8.1858
Ashurst, Lieut. C.H.	2.2.1878

Beavan, Lieut. H.M.	18.4.1878
Beynon (Benyon), Captain W.H. (late 23rd Regt)	20.4.1878
Bolland, Lieut. C.J.	15.4.1874
Chapman, Captain & Adjutant W. (late Rifle Bde)	28.3.1829
Churchill, Lieut. R.	25.9.1808
Duff, Captain C.G.	8.4.1875
Ellis, Ens. J.R.	23.3.1809
Evans, Lieut. O.L.J.	7.2.1877
Hogg, Lieut. J.D.M.	28.1.1879
Huddart, Lieut. A.K.	15.3.1876
Hughes, Ens. H.	10.4.1812
Jones, Ens. O.M.	20.4.1854
Kearney, Lieut. D.O.	2.5.1806
Lovell, Lieut. H.W.	14.5.1876
Lloyd, Ens. H.	25.6.1812
Lloyd, Lieut. J.E.	4.2.1839
Mostyn, Lieut. H.R.H. Lloyd	22.9.1875
Parry, Captain T.P.J.	25.12.1805
Peel, Lieut. H.L.	15.4.1874
Pennant, Lieut. G.S.D.	29.10.1856
Platt, Lieut. J.H.	15.3.1876
Price, Lieut. T.S.	25.9.1810
Riddell, Lieut. H.E.B.	7.2.1877
Roberts, Lieut. C.N.	20.6.1877
Roberts, Lieut. T.E.	10.7.1838
Robson, Ens. J.	17.10.1808
Rowley, Cao. C.G.E. (late 23rd Regt)	28.8.1879

Carnarvon Militia — Return of Strength dated 25th June, 1822
Permanent Staff

Staff Sergeants	1
Sergeants	3
Corporals	3
Buglers	1

Disembodied Strength

Privates	68
Wanting to complete	60 Privates

(4. R.W.F. Records)

THE MILITIA BARRACKS

The Militia Barracks, Caernarfon, was built on a field known as Cae Bach on the outskirts of the town and which was sold to the County for that purpose in 1854 by the Vaynol Estate.

The Armoury and the Barracks was built in the following year at a cost of £4,069.18.11.

In 1882 the property was leased to the War Office for 99 years at an annual rent of £60.10.0 — a nominal sum, engineered by the War Office under threat of withdrawing the Militia Headquarters from the County.

In 1910, the Barracks was re-leased to the Carnarvonshire Territorial Force Association for a term of 50 years which lease expired in 1960. Prior to that date, after prolonged negotiations, the Territorial and Auxiliary Forces Association for the Counties of Anglesey and Caernarfonshire were able to arrange an outright purchase of the establishment, which business was completed on May 1st, 1961. The buildings, well preserved, are still in use today.

SOLDIERS OF THE 4th BATTALION, ROYAL WELCH FUSILIERS, WHO DIED OR WERE KILLED IN ACTION DURING THE SOUTH AFRICAN WAR 1899-1902

EVANS, 1787, Private William — Killed in action	24.10.1900
GELDER, 1812, Private George — Drowned	19.4.1901
JONES, 2480, Private John — Killed in Action with the Devons	21.1.1901
KELLY, 2554, Private William — Died	8.6.1902
MAILEN, 2823, Private Thomas — Died	13.5.1900
NOLAN, 1621, Private John — Killed in Action	9.10.1900
TAYLOR, 1775, Private Frederick — Killed in Action with the Devons	24.12.1900
WILLIAMS, 2681, Private William Henry — Died	15.11.1900
THOMAS, 2829, Private Hugh — Killed in Action with the Devons	22.2.1901
WALSH, 1976, Private James — Killed in Action with the Devons	24.8.1901

COLOURS

The Colours issued to the Corps in the period 1762 to 1812 would have been of standard dimension for Infantry Colours, viz: — 6′ on the Pole and 6′6″ in the fly.

The 1st or King's Colour was the Great Union, the design of which was changed in 1801 due to the Act of Union, to include the Cross of St. Patrick. The King's Colour issued to the Regiment c.1804 would therefore have included this change.

The 2nd or Regimental Colour for the same period would have been of similar dimensions and be made of blue silk[1] to match the Facing Colour of the Regiment.

That issued in 1762 would have had as its motif, the Arms of the Lord Lieutenant, the 1st Baron Newborough, which Heraldry is described as follows: Sa, three Fleur de Lis, arg. Crest-A Dexter cubit Arm erect, in Armour, holding in the hand, ppr, a Fleur de Lis, or.

Supporters — Two Lions, gu., the dexter gorged with a Collar, or, charged with three Fleur de Lis, sa; the sinister, with a collar, arg, charged with three crosses-formee, gu.

Motto — Suaviter in Modo, Fortiter in Re. (Gentle in Manner, but Vigorous in Deed). Additionally, the top canton nearest the Pole would contain the Union design. It is very likely that the design described remained unchanged up until c.1804, in which year the Colours of the Regiment were replaced.

Preserved in the Regimental Museum of The Royal Welch Fusiliers at Caernarfon are two Militia Colours, namely those carried by the County Militia in the period c.1804 to 1812. These relics had been laid up for many years in the Garrison Church of the town, but were recently removed to the Museum due to the inability of the Church authorities to guarantee their preservation.

The 1st or King's Colour consists of the Great Union and of similar dimensions to its predecessor. Its condition, considering the amount of time it has been exposed to light and dust is fair, with only small patches of Silk falling away on the fly. It will however require the attention of a Textile Conservation Officer if it is desired to preserve it for many more years.

The 2nd or Regimental Colour was originally a blue silk flag with the Union Flag in the top Canton nearest the Pole and, at the centre, a closed Union Wreath of intertwined Roses, Shamrock and Thistle in the appropriate embroidered thread. Within the Wreath, in gold embroidered letters, the Regimental title in three parts, one over the other — 'ROYAL CARNARVON MILITIA'.

The condition of this Colour is poor in the extreme, with the Colours badly faded and the silk fabric crumbling away from the net. The design is however still visible, and my already expressed opinion is that it can be preserved for many years yet, if proper restorative action is taken without delay.

The Regiment, on being converted to a Rifle Corps in 1812, ceased to carry

Colours, the Stand thereafter being preserved in the Militia Store and later Barracks erected in Caernarfon. That the Colours were in the Store in 1840 is confirmed by the following note from the Records of Service of the 4th R.W.F.

"H.Q. Carnarvon,
10th February, 1840.
The Sergeant Major and Sergeants will be in Regimentals by 11 o' clock and be at the Stores at half past eleven for the Colours, and with a party of the 23rd Royal Welch Fusiliers, troop the Colours through the Town as far as Bryn Helen, and then lodge them at the Sportsman Hotel."

Finally, the Colours presented to the 4th (Militia) Battalion, Royal Welsh Fusiliers in 1885 were of the smaller 1858 design — 4′ on the Pole and 4′6″ in the Fly. In appearance both look very similar to those carried by the Regular Battalions of the Royal Welsh Fusiliers in the same period. Following the disbandment of the 4th Bn on March 31st, 1908, the following instructions were received regarding their disposal.

"From Director of Equipment and Ordnance Stores,
To the Officer Commanding 4th R.W.F.
I am directed to inform you that approval is hereby given for the Colours of the 4th Royal Welsh Fusiliers to be deposited in Christchurch, at Carnarvon."

Footnote

1. W.Y. Carman, Esq., recollects sighting one reference, the source of which has unfortunately been misplaced, which for 1762 describes the 2nd or Regimental Colour of the Regiment as Arms of the Lord Lieutenant on a white ground.

REGIMENTAL COLOUR — CARNARVONSHIRE MILITIA 1803-1812

(Owen Collection)

UNIFORM DRESS

The Dress of both Officers and Other Ranks was similar to that worn by their counterparts in the red coated Infantry of the Line, i.e., from 1762 to 1812 — Red with Blue Facings.

c.1780, the Osborn Book, already mentioned describes the Coat as being Red with Blue Facings and White (Silver) Lace.

In 1799, the *British Military Journal* gives: Facings Blue. Officers Silver Epaulette. In 1812 on conversion to a Rifle Corps the Uniform was changed to Rifle Green. Hamilton Smith's Chart, 1814, indicates a dark green coat and breeches with black collar and cuffs, silver lace and buttons. About 1862, the Facings were changed from Black to Red, a shade described in 1867 as Scarlet. From that date through to 1881 the colour of Uniform Dress and Facings remained unchanged. A Letter dated 18th December, 1822, confirms the Rifle Green shade:

"Sir,

Colonel Edwards has transmitted to me your Letter of the 10th inst. He desires me to inform you that the Clothing of the Permanent Staff of the Regiment is to be supplied from the Public Stores. The size Roll enclosed to you in my letter of the 4th, will I hope answer your every purpose, and I beg leave to mention that the colour of the Uniform is Green, the same as the Rifle Brigade.

I, have the honour, etc., etc.,

G.T. Sewell. (Captain & Adjutant)."

In 1881, the Corps having amalgamated with the Royal Merioneth Rifles to form the 4th Battalion, Royal Welsh Fusiliers, the Uniform Dress was changed to that of the parent regiment. Red Tunics with Blue Facings were taken into use, with the distinguishing letter 'M' on the Shoulder Strap. The Lace worn by the Officers was silver.

MILITIAMAN
LIGHT COMPANY,
c.1780

MILITIAMAN
GRENADIER
COMPANY, c.1780

(Battalion Coys) c.1780

By kind permission of W.Y. Carman, Esq., and Lord Danvers Osborn

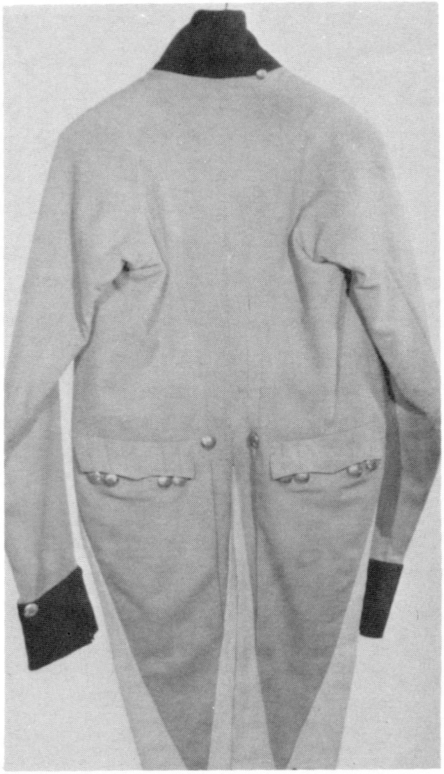

AN OFFICERS REGIMENTAL COAT,
ROYAL CARNARVONSHIRE MILITIA, c.1803
By kind permission of Christie's of Kensington

BADGES AND BUTTONS

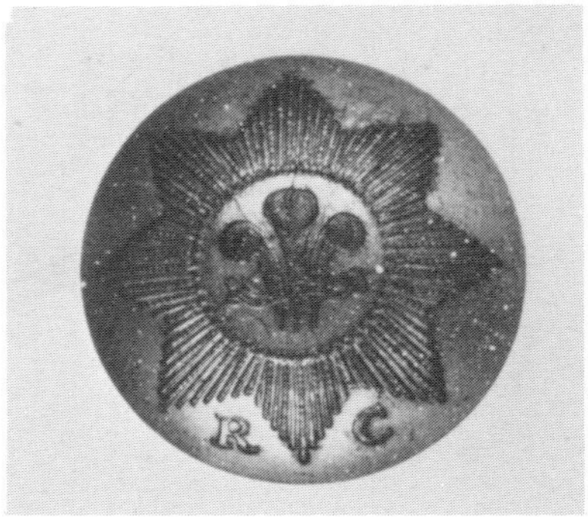

Officers Coatee Button, Royal Carnarvon Militia c.1803
Gilt, Convex, Open backed and 20mm in diameter.
On the face the design of the Plumes, Coronet and Motto of the Prince of Wales within a rayed Star of eight points. Below the star the letter 'R.C.'
Owen Collection

BADGE CAP, OTHER RANKS PATTERN, c.1854
A Stringed Bugle Horn over a scroll inscribed 'ROYAL CARNARVON'
A two part bugle in blackened brass.
Owen Collection

ROYAL CARNARVON RIFLES.
POUCH BELT PLATE, OFFICERS PATTERN,
c.1858

A Maltese Cross with Lions set between the limbs and with points culminating in a decorative ball or orb. Superimposed at the centre of the Cross, a circle enclosing the raised title 'ROYAL CARNARVON RIFLES'. Inside the circle on a voided ground, the Plumes, Coronet and Motto of the Prince of Wales. The whole in balckened metal.

By kind permission of Dr J. Carey Hughes.

PLATE. SHAKO. OFFICERS PATTERN.
c.1858

A Maltese Cross surmounted by a blank Plinth and Victorian Crown. At the centre a circle enclosing the raised title 'ROYAL CARNARVON RIFLES'. Inside the circle, the Plumes, Coronet and Motto Scrolls of the Prince of Wales. The whole in blackened metal.

By kind permission of Dr J. Carey Hughes.

PLATE SHAKO, OFFICERS PATTERN, c.1878
A Maltese Cross with Lions between the Limbs and surmounted by a Victorian Crown. At the centre of the Cross a Circle enclosing the raised title 'ROYAL CARNARVON RIFLE MILITIA'. Inside the Circle a Bugle Horn enclosing the Regimental Precedence Number 56 between the Strings.
The whole in blackened metal.

At least 6 of these Plates are known to exist and are held by Private Collectors and the R.W.F. Museum.
Owen Collection

ROYAL CARNARVON AND ANGLESEY RIFLES
SHAKO PLATE, OFFICERS PATTERN, c.1865

A Maltese Cross with blank plinth surmounted by the Victorian Crown. At the centre a circle enclosing the title 'ROYAL CARNARVON AND ANGLESEY RIFLES'. Within the circle, a stringed Bugle Horn of the Light Infantry pattern. The whole in bronzed or blacked brass.

By kind permission of Dr J. Carey Hughes

Note: A Badge of this pattern is held by the Museum of Welsh Antiquities, Bangor. The Badge is damaged, as the Crown above the plinth is missing. It was the gift of Miss Lloyd of Bath to the Museum.

THE MILITIA LONG SERVICE MEDAL

Eight Militia Long Service Medals were awarded to men of the 4th Battalion, Royal Welsh Fusiliers.

THE PROVISIONAL CAVALRY, 1796-1801

Very little is recorded concerning the activities of this Cavalry Force which was established by Act 37, Geo 111 of 1796. Intended as an additional aid to home defence, the scheme was from its inception unpopular, and did not receive willingly the support of the landowning Class or from others who owned and made use of horses as part of their daily business. The Act required the provision of one Provisional Cavalryman, fully clothed and accoutred, and with suitably furnished mount, by every person owning ten horses on which duty was paid. Those owning less than ten, were to join with others similarly situated to provide likewise. The man selected to serve as a Provisional Cavalryman was to be selected by ballot, and when embodied, would be entitled to military pay. Such a man was required to take the Oath of Allegiance, and would be subject to certain penalties if he failed to turn out for exercise, or did so improperly equipped.

So unpopular was this Act that, within the course of that same year, it was amended to produce a more acceptable compromise. By the amending Act, the Lords Lieutenant who could provide as Volunteers, three quarters of the Provisional Cavalry quota required from their counties, were empowered to dispense with the Provisional Cavalry Ballot and provide instead a Troop or Troops of Yeomanry Cavalry.

That the Act was enforced in Caernarfonshire is supported by a document contained in the Porth yr Aur MSS, held by the University College of North Wales, Bangor. The Document, No.2859, gives details of the expenses agreed upon at a General Meeting of the Lieutenancy to discuss ways and means of meeting the requirements of the Act.

"To the Principal balloted to provide a Substitute to attend the general muster	£5-0-0
For cloathing every man	£2-9-6
For a Principal balloted for providing a Horse to be approved for that purpose	£13-13-0
For providing the furniture for the Horse, and Spurs	£4-0-0
For extra expenses in maintaining and keeping the Horse for the Service for one year	£5-0-0
For maintaining and keeping the Horse per day for every day such Horse is out, in going to, attending, or returning from muster	1-6

Fortescue states that part of the Provisional Cavalry Force was embodied in 1797 and remained in service until 1800.[1] No record of such embodiment taking place in Anglesey or Caernarfonshire, or for that matter, any Welsh County has been found, but the document above quoted implies that in Caernarfonshire, Provisional Cavalrymen mustered for training, and no doubt similar arrangements were made in Anglesey. An Act of 1798 made provision to embody part of the Force for training, as a result of which the Provisional Cavalry in several Welsh Counties complied. Although not listed amongst them, one must assume that the Provisional Cavalry of Anglesey and Caernarfonshire did likewise, there being no loophole such as the existance of a Troop of Yeomanry Cavalry in either county which would allow the respective Lords Lieutenant to avoid that responsibility.

The disembodiment of Militia and Auxiliary Forces which came with the Peace of 1801 saw the last of the unpopular body which was summed up by a politician as follows:

"The Provisional Cavalry passed over the county like a blight. It was a pleasant conceit to make every man mount another man's horse, till at length, when all the men and horses were brought together, no man knew how to mount, and so they all separated."[2]

Footnotes

1. Fortescue, History of The British Army, Vol IV, Part 2. p.891
2. Ditto.

THE VOLUNTEER MOVEMENT
1794-1802 and 1803-1808

The year 1794 found Great Britain at War with the traditional enemy, France, and with the Government of the day justifiably alarmed at the extensive military preparations then taking place on the French Channel coast: activities directed towards an invasion of the British shore. The situation was in many ways similar to that which our Country faced one hundred and fortysix years later, when in 1940, the British stood alone facing the armed might of Hitler's Germany across the same narrow strip of sea.

With the comparatively small Regular Army heavily committed to foreign service, and the responsibility for Home Defence mainly in the hands of an understrength and inexperienced Militia, it became clear that a rapid augmentation of the Land Forces available to resist Invasion was long overdue. In consequence the Government gave some serious thought to the matter.

On March 5th, 1794, the Prime Minister, Mr Pitt, laid before the House certain proposals, the outcome of which was an Act,[1] which not only included measures for strengthening the Militia, but also authorised the raising, at comparatively low cost to Government, of Volunteer Corps of all arms for the purpose of Local and National Defence.

Although somewhat slow in gaining momentum, the response in Wales was considerable after 1797 — spurred on, no doubt, by the news of the abortive French Invasion of West Pembrokeshire in February of that year. The reaction is described by an eminent military historian — "There sprang up an infinity of Volunteer Corps, Infantry, Artillery, and Light Horse or Yeomanry Cavalry, first in single Companies and Troops, but very soon in Battalions and Regiments."[2]

Clause 31 of the Act aimed to "Encourage and discipline such Corps and companies of men as shall voluntarily enrol themselves for the defence of their Counties, Towns and Coasts, or for the general defence of the Kingdom."

It provided that any Corps of Volunteers which had been raised by Officers commissioned by the King, or by the Lord Lieutenant of a County, or by a person authorised by the King, which in the event of invasion or riot, assembled to march on the King's service, would receive pay as for Regular Troops and be subject to military discipline. In return, such Volunteers would be exempted from the liability to serve in the Militia and also receive certain other privileges.

Armed with Muskets and Pikes, or a mixture of both, the Infantry Volunteer Corps received little official assistance. Weapons were promised, but being slow to materialise from Government arsenals, were often acquired privately. Uniform Dress was likewise difficult to obtain, and for the less affluent units was often a mixture of Regular Army or Militia cast offs. At the other end of the scale, however, were Volunteers better armed and dressed than the Regulars, but solely due to the fact that they were sponsored by either wealthy landowners or industrialists. Such men spared no expense on the new hobby, and vied with each other in producing the best dressed and most efficient unit.

It would be pleasant to believe (as was true in many cases) that patriotism was the spur behind those who came forward to serve. Sadly the movement was used as a means of avoiding the Militia Ballot, not only by individuals, but also by Landowners and wealthy sponsors, who found in the Volunteer Force a suitable means of retaining, free from the threat of the Press or other inconvenient form of military service, their best employees, and so protected from the demands of a country at war their own selfish financial interests.

This first phase of Volunteer activity ended with the Peace of Amiens in 1802, in which year the Volunteer Corps, with the exception of certain Corps of Yeomanry Cavalry were disbanded.

To clarify matters relating to Volunteer Corps of that first period, one must also mention here the Defence of the Realm Act of 1798. The Act required the Lords Lieutenant to compile lists of all able bodied men between the ages of 15 and 60 for defence of all kinds, together with details of their occupation, and stipulating the type of service, combatant or non-combatant, which they would be capable of rendering in time of emergency. The Act resulted in the formation of Armed Associations, in which persons of a community so registered, could unite to form bands of 50 men, primarily for Local Defence, and whose administration would be the responsibility of a locally elected Committee, and whose Officers would be selected by ballot of the local inhabitants. The essential difference between these Associations and the various Corps of Cavalry, Infantry and Artillery Volunteers was that the former also made use of non-combatant men, who for reasons of age or other circumstances, could not, or preferred not to bear Arms. Such men were made Constables, responsible for marshalling, prior to evacuation, of civilians, stores, livestock and other useful material. Others were made Look-outs, Beacon Watchers and Drivers for requisitioned Waggons. Sadly, many of the Associations raised in Wales were not officially listed, and are only found by search of contemporary news-sheets and locally preserved documents. It would appear however, that several of the Welsh Infantry Volunteer Corps first sprang into existence in the guise of the Armed Association. The Levee en Masse Lists, such as have survived, are most useful to the Family Historian, and are found mainly in Private, Parish or Borough Records.

In January 1803, it became clear that the flimsy peace signed at Amiens would not much longer survive, and in preparation for approaching War with France, the Government on March 11th issued orders to embody the Militia. This was followed on March 31st by a call for the revival of the Volunteer Force under terms outlined in a Volunteer Act of 1802. A Circular Letter addressed to the various Lords Lieutenant gave details of the terms of service, and a promise of support from Government somewhat more generous than had been extended to them prior to 1802. The response, as before, was considerable, and Government in an attempt to regulate the size of the Volunteer Force, stipulated that the number of Volunteers raised in any County was to be limited to a figure, six times that of its authorised Militia Quota. That Quota for both Anglesey and Caernarfonshire was 128, hence the number of Volunteers allowed for each County was limited to 768. Where additional numbers were desirable, they could serve as Supernumenaries, and as such would not be entitled to exemption from the Militia Ballot or receive Pay, Allowances or Privileges. In Caernarfonshire, the Loyal Newborough Supernumenaries provide an example of that form of service.

By December 1803, there were nationally (excluding Ireland) some 380,000[3] Volunteers under arms, and depending on the date of formation of a Corps and the type of service which its members were prepared to render, received from Government financial and other support of one of two categories. Known as the June and August Allowances, it is not proposed to explain their intricacies here. Sufficient to say that both Anglesey and Carnarvonshire Volunteers received the August Allowances in return for which they were allowed Pay for 20 days. In return for the financial support they were required in the event of Invasion, or the appearance of an enemy in force off the coast, to march to defend any part of Great Britain.

The whole or greater part of the paid training period was invariably devoted to what was termed 'Permanent Duty' i.e., a period of training cum Garrison duty either alone or in Battalion or Brigade in towns around the County and neighbouring Counties. Such training was similar in many ways to the Annual Camps which are attended by the Territorial Army of the present day. During such periods, the Volunteer soldiers, as was the custom of the day, were billeted in the Inns and common Lodging houses of the town. Whilst engaged on such duties, the conduct of the Volunteers was generally far superior to that of Regular troops, as bad behaviour could lead, in addition to a military penalty, to unemployment, dimissal from the Corps, and consequent loss of protection from the Naval Press Gang, Army Recruiters and the Militia Ballot. That the Volunteers were smart, and often highly efficient, is borne out by Inspection Reports, the authors of which, General Officers and Inspecting Field Officers, were not often given to giving praise unless it was merited.

The Victory at Trafalgar in October, 1805, removed for the duration of the war the threat of invasion. Napoleon's Army of England was diverted to other campaigns, and the problem then for Britain became one of maintaining her Regular Army at full strength. In furthering that aim, it soon became clear that the large Volunteer Force was a serious encumberance, as the exemption and protection which it gave its members reflected seriously on the numbers and quality of men available for the regular service. The establishment had no great objection to Gentlemen, and men of some means claiming those privileges whilst "playing the Soldier",[4] but it came to object most strongly to Artisans and men of the Labouring Class claiming the same immunity. A part answer to the problem came in 1807 with the passing of the Local Militia

Act, which new Force came into being the following year. It sounded the death knell for the Volunteer Force with the exception of Yeomanry Cavalry. Allowances, Privileges and other forms of Government support were withdrawn, and although some units carried on for a while at their own expense, by 1812, the Volunteer Infantry arm was dead, and had been replaced by Regiments of Local Militia.

No Volunteer Corps in Anglesey or Caernarfonshire appears to have survived the change, the majority of those serving electing to transfer voluntarily into the Local Militia.

The demise of the Volunteer Force was estimated to have saved the country not less than £109,000 per annum, and more important released a considerable part of the active male population for selection during future Militia Ballots[5]

Footnotes

1. Act 34 Geo 111, c.31
2. Fortescue. Hon. J.W., The History of the British Army
3. Returns. Volunteers of the United Kingdom
   Ordered by House of Commons to be printed 9th & 13th December, 1803,
   Revised to February, 1804.
4. William Windham, War Secretary
   see 'The Defenders', G. Cousins, Frederick Muller, London, 1968
5. Cambrian April 2nd, 1813.

VOLUNTEERS
1797-1802
ANGLESEY

LOYAL ANGLESEA VOLUNTEERS 1797-1802

Raised by Viscount Bulkeley, the Corps was accepted for service on the 5th July, 1797, with Thomas Bulkeley as Captain Commandant.

By October, the Corps numbered 3 Companies and was dressed in a fashion similar to that worn by the Regular Regiments of the Line, viz, a Red Coat which had blue Facings.

It is known that the unit was often unofficially and incorrectly referred to as the 'ROYAL ANGLESEA VOLUNTEERS' and went so far as to include on some of its insignia the incorrect prefix 'ROYAL'. By the end of 1788 the Corps numbered four Companies and remained at that strength until its disbandment in 1802.

Officers serving as at c.June, 1799 were:

Thomas, Viscount Bulkeley of Beaumaris[1]	Major Commandant	11 October, 1797
Owen P. Meyrick of Bodorgan	Captain	5 July, 1797
John Lewis	Captain	7 December, 1797
Holland Griffith	Captain	20 June, 1798
Herbert Jones of Llynon[2]	Lieut.	5 July, 1797
William Meyrick	Lieut.	5 July, 1797
Hugh Evans	Lieut.	20 June, 1798
Hugh Wynne[3]	Lieut.	3 May, 1799
Holland Griffith (Jnr)	2nd Lieut.	5 July, 1797
Robert Bulkeley	2nd Lieut.	5 July, 1797
William Sparrow[4]	2nd Lieut.	5 July, 1797
Robert Pritchard	2nd Lieut.	20 June, 1798

LOYAL PARIS MOUNTAIN VOLUNTEERS 1797-1802

Raised by Captain John Price from the labour force employed in the Parys Mountain Copper Mines near Amlwch, first mention of the Corps is made in the *Hereford Journal* of August 1797.

No record of the unit can be found in any of the Army or Volunteer Lists of the period, but further proof of its existence can be found amongst documents included in the Plas Newydd MSS held in the University College of North Wales, Bangor.

Those documents contain a Return dated 25th December, 1799, which show that the Corps at that date consisted of two Companies organised as follows:

1st Company	**2nd Company**
Captain John Price	Captaincy vacant
Lieut. John Palmer	Lieut. and Adjutant Theophilus Jones
Lieut. John Price	Ensign Robert Petters
Ensign John Evans	Ensign Richard Broadhead
Sgt. Major John Robyns	
	10 Sergeants
10 Sergeants	6 Corporals
7 Corporals	2 Drummers
2 Drummers	2 Fifers
2 Fifers	101 Privates
104 Privates	

A later Return for December 1800 lists Officers as

1st Company	**2nd Company**
Captain John Price	Captain Theophilus Jones
Lieut. George Palmer	Lieut. Robert Peters
2nd Lieut. William Hughes	2nd Lieut. John Evans
Ensign John Paynter	Ensign John Owen

Theophilus Jones is noted as being promoted Captain, vice Captain Parks (deceased)

Footnotes

1. Thomas James, 7th Viscount, Born 1752, Died 1822
2. High Sheriff of Anglesey 1791
3. Of Beaumaris. High Sheriff of Anglesey, 1799
4. Probably William Bodychan Sparrow of Tŷ-Newydd, High Sheriff 1822

PLATE. SHOULDER BELT, OFFICER.
LOYAL ANGLESEY VOLUNTEERS, c.1797
An oval silver plate with roped rim. Around the edge of the plate in raised letters the title 'LOYAL ANGLESEA VOLUNTEERS 1797'.
At the centre the raised design of the Plumes, Coronet and Motto of the Prince of Wales.
(National Army Museum Collection) Acc. No. 6612.12
It is likely that the Plate continued in use by Officers of the Corps in the period 1803-1808.

PLATE. CROSS BELT.
LOYAL ANGLESEA VOLUNTEERS, c.1797
An oval brass plate with traces of gilt. Engraved around the rim the title 'ROYAL ANGLESEA VOLUNTEERS 1797'. At the centre the engraved device of the Plumes, Coronet and Motto of the Prince of Wales.
The use of the prefix 'Royal' is probably the result of a manufacturers error, as the Corps was in no sense of the word a 'ROYAL' regiment.
(J. Tyler Collection)

MEDAL SILVER SHOOTING. ANGLESEY VOLUNTEER INFANTRY, 1801
A silver prize medal for shooting, the obverse engraved with the motif of the Plumes, Coronet and Motto of the Prince of Wales between the letters G.R. Above the Plumes, the title 'ANGLESEY VOLUNTEERS'. Below the Plumes, Laurel sprays and the date 1801. The reverse is inscribed 'PRIZE SHOOTING MEDAL OF THE HOLYHEAD COMPANY WON BY SERGT. DANIEL EVANS'
(Haythornthwaite Records)

The Medal is also described by D. Hastings Irwin in 'War Medals and Decorations', London, 4th Edition, 1910.

VOLUNTEERS 1795-1802
CAERNARFONSHIRE

CAERNARFONSHIRE YEOMANRY CAVALRY

At a meeting held in the Grand Jury Room, Caernarfon, on January 24th, 1795, it was resolved that a Corps of Gentlemen and Yeomanry be raised in the County as a general contribution to the internal defence of the country.

Benson Freeman, RNR, in No.38 of his series of articles on the Historical Records of the Yeomanry Regiments[1] opines that such a Corps was raised, but in the absence of any other information additional to an account of the Meeting above mentioned it would appear unlikely that the matter proceeded any further than the disucssion stage.

Footnotes

Volunteer Services Gazette

CARNARVON VOLUNTEER ASSOCIATION 1798-1802

Raised by Captain Richard Garnons of Pantdu, Llanllyfni, one time Lieutenant in the 79th Foot,[1] the Corps consisted of one Company (approx. 60-100 men)

Other Officers gazetted with Richard Garnons on the 5th July, 1798, were

1st Lieutenant James Butler
2nd Lieutenant Owen Anthony Poole[2]
2nd Lieutenant Glynne Griffith[3]

Nothing is known regarding the Uniform Dress and distinctions worn by this Corps, but there exists a Good Shooting Medal awarded in 1800 which is inscribed "The Gift of the Company Officers adjudged by the vote of the members of 'A' Company to Sergeant John Williamson for his good shooting."

EIFIONYDD VOLUNTEER ASSOCIATION 1798-1802

Raised in July 1798, even less is known about the activities of this small Corps which consisted of a Company of approximately 60 men under the command of Lieut. John Williams (gazetted 5th July, 1798)

LOYAL NEWBOROUGH VOLUNTEER ASSOCIATION 1799-1802

Raised on the 28th October, 1799, the founder of this strong and well equipped Volunteer Corps was Thomas, Lord Newborough,[4] who was also its Lieut. Colonel Commandant.

Numbering six Companies, the Corps was clothed in Scarlet Jackets with blue Facings — a form of dress similar to that worn by the Regular Infantry of the day. The letter sanctioning the Corps reads as follows: "To Our Right Trusty and Wellbeloved, Thomas, Lord Newborough, Greetings:

We do by these Presents constitute and appoint you to be during our pleasure, Lieut. Coll, Commandant of the Loyal Association — Association of the inhabitants of the coast of the County of Carnarvon, associated to serve without Pay, for the Protection thereof, in the Case of any Emergency, at the Requisition of the Civil Power; but not to take rank in our Army, nor the said Association to be subject to Military Discipline, or to serve out of the said County, except of their own accord. Given at our Court at St. James's, the Twenty-eighth Day of October, 1799, in the Fortieth Year of Our Reign.

By His Majesty's command
Signed
Portland."[5]

The late E. Alfred Jones, M.A., F.S.A., refers to this unit in one of his articles[6] as the 'Royal Carnarvonshire Grenadiers'. It is my opinion that in doing so, he confused the Volunteer Corps with the County Militia, another of Lord Newborough's responsibilities, but the reader must draw his or her own conclusions on that point.

Headquarters of the Loyal Newborough was a Fort called Fort Williamsburg situated in the grounds of Glynllifon Park, and also, close by, Fort Belan on the shores of the Menai Straits. The former building also appears to have been used as a store by the Permanent Staff of the County Militia. During the winter of 1800-01 the Newborough Corps assembled in readiness to act in Aid of the Civil Power during a period of unrest amongst Slate Quarrymen in the County.[7] Fortunately the situation did not deteriorate sufficiently to require such intervention.

In 1935, there was preserved in the old Fort at Glynllifon a Regimental Colour carried by this Corps which bore in addition to the Arms of Wynne of Glynllifon, a scroll inscribed 'Loyal Newborough Association'. Also preserved in the Fort at that date were many Muskets, items of Uniform Dress and various categories of military accoutrement. The Drum of the Association, together with a Stand of Muskets and miscellaneous Accountrements were c.1979 displayed at Fort Belan, but have since been removed by the Newborough family. Some of the Pouches displayed Artillery ornaments which suggests that a proportion of the men were trained as Gunners in order to man the various pieces mounted in the Fort. Preserved in the Museum of The Royal Welch Fusiliers in Caernarfon Castle is an example of the Cross Belt Plate worn by the Corps. The oval copper plate which was at one time gilded has engraved upon its face the intertwined letters 'L.N.A.' set below a Georgian Crown and the Cipher 'GR'. The letter 'G' of the Royal Cipher is placed on the left of the Crown and the letter 'R' on its right.

The Buttons worn by Officers of the Corps were gilt, convex and open backed and had as motif an eight pointed star. Within the star and at its centre, a circle containing the letters L.N.A.A. (Loyal Newborough Armed Association). The Corps in common with other Caernarfonshire Volunteer bodies stood down in 1802.

This Corps and its 1803 successor must not be confused with the unofficial Volunteer Corps which Sir Thomas Wynne raised from amongst his friends and associates in 1761, and which was styled 'The Society or Garrison of Fort Williamsburg'. That unit was a purely private venture, and more inclined towards social than military activities. It had no official recoginition as far as is known, and does not appear in any Army List of that period.

PENRHYN VOLUNTEERS, 1798-1802

Raised by Captain John Jones, this small Corps consisted of one Company and was accepted for service on the 24 June, 1798. It was also referred to as the 'Llanlledryd and Llandegai Volunteer Association' in the news-sheets of the day, but very little else is known concerning its members or activities.

PWLLHELI VOLUNTEER ASSOCIATION 1798-1802

Known also as the 'Loyal Pwllheli Volunteers' and 'Llanor and Denio Volunteers' this small Corps of one Company strength was raised by Captain William Griffith of Rhosfawr.

Accepted for service on the 24th June, 1798, other Officers gazetted were 1st Lieutenant Griffith Tomas and 2nd Lieutenant John Ellis. E. Alfred Jones, in an article already referred to, describes the Commanding Officer as an Attorney at Law and states that he was appointed to command the Llanor and Denio Volunteers on the 15th June, 1798. He also states that c.1935, a Cross Belt Plate to this Corps was in the possession of the family then resident in Nanhoron. It was described as being made of copper and inscribed with the Cipher of George III.

LLANDUDNO VOLUNTEERS 1798-1802

No mention of the existance or composition of this Corps has been found. In the Royal Welch Fusiliers Museum at Caernarfon Castle is preserved a

Medal of Merit. In gold, the Medal is inscribed 'Award of Merit to Henry Lewis, Esq., as a token of his efficiency in the cause of the Llandudno Volunteers, 12th July, 1801.'

Footnotes

1. later Queen's Own Cameron Highlanders
2. A Caernarfon Solicitor and Clerk of the Peace for the County
3. Eldest Son of William Griffith of Rhosfawr and Bodegroes, nr Pwllheli and an Attorney at Law with chambers in Caernarfon
4. Thomas Wynne of Glynllifon
5. Article. The Society or Garrison of Fort Williamsburg. E.A. Jones, M.A., F.S.A., Y Cymmrodor, Vol XLIV. 1935
6. See Footnote 5
7. Y Cymmordor. Vol XLIV. 1935 (see Footnote 5)

The Medal of the Carnarvon Volunteer Association is described by D. Hastings Irwin in 'War Medals and Decorations', London, 4th Edition, 1910.

Cross Belt Plate — Universal Pattern worn
by armed associations, c.1798
Brass with engraved lettering.
(Owen Collection)

VOLUNTEERS
1803-1808
Anglesey

On being reformed in 1803, the Anglesey Volunteers were organised into two Battalions. Many of those who came forward to serve had prior to 1802 been members of Loyal Anglesey and Paris Mountain Volunteers which stood down after the Peace of Amiens.

ANGLESEY LOYAL VOLUNTEER INFANTRY
1803-1808

Raised in 1803, the Corps was accepted for service on the 12th October under the command of Colonel, The Viscount Bulkeley of Beaumaris.

The unit comprised 2 Battalions with establishment:

2 Field Officers
5 Captains
3 Staff Officers
15 Subalterns
26 Sergeants
5 Drummers
500 Privates

the whole wearing a Uniform similar to that worn by the Infantry of the Line consisting of a Red Coat with Blue Facings and White Breeches. The Officers' Coats were plain, no Lace being worn.

The Plas Coch MSS contain Muster Rolls of Sir W. Bulkeley Hughes' Company for 1804 and 1805
Captain Sir W. Bulkeley Hughes[1]
1st Lieutenant W. Price
2nd Lieutenant W. Thomas
Ensign Richard Lewis.
Additionally listed are 5 Sergeants, 4 Corporals and 94 Privates. The List of Officers for 1805 remains unchanged, as also the number of Sergeants, otherwise there were 5 Corporals, 2 Drummers and 95 Privates.

In June 1804, the Corps assembled for a period a Permanent Duty at Beaumaris during which their good conduct earned the public thanks of the Mayor and inhabitants of the town.

In May/June 1805 the 1st Battalion assembled at Beaumaris for 14 days Permanent Duty, and the 2nd Battalion at Caernarfon for a similar period — a pattern repeated through to 1808. During the training period, the 1st Battalion was presented with "a pair of elegant Colours",[2] the presentation being made by a Mrs Peacoke,[3] deputising for the donor, the Countess of Uxbridge.

Both Battalions are reported to have conducted themselves in an exemplary manner during training, and received the thanks of the townspeople of Beaumaris and Caernarfon prior to their dismissal.[4] By January 1809, both Battalions had been disbanded, the majority of the Officers and Other Ranks having transferred their services into the newly formed Regiment of Anglesey Local Militia.

The Cambrian[5] records that prior to disbandment, the Officers and Other Ranks of the 2nd Battalion presented their Major, Bodychan Sparrow, Esq., with a piece of Plate, value £60, as a token of their respect and appreciation.

No record of Colours being presented to the 2nd Battalion has been found, but it is almost certain that they did receive Colours at some date between 1803 and 1805.

The Colours of the 1st Battalion do not appear to have survived through to the present day.

Footnotes

1. Sir W. Bulkeley Hughes, Kt of Plas Coch
2. Cambrian 14th June, 1805
3. Possibly the Wife of the Lieut. Colonel Peacoke who commanded the Anglesey Militia without much distinction, c.1780
4. Cambrian 14th June, 1805
5. Cambrian September 29th, 1809

D. Hastings Irwin in 'War Medals and Decorations' 4th Edition, 1910, describes a Shooting Medal awarded to William Vaughan of the Beaumaris Volunteer Infantry (i.e., the Beaumaris Company of the Loyal Anglesey)
Observe: An Armorial Design
Reverse: engraved 'Best shot of the Company, 1804, William Vaughan'.

VOLUNTEERS
1803-1808
CAERNARFONSHIRE

LOYAL CARNARVON MERCANTILE VOLUNTEERS 1803-1804

Raised by Thomas Assheton Smith of Vaynol, the services of this Corps were accepted on the 7th October, 1803

The Uniform Dress worn by this Corps was similar to that worn by Line Infantry and consisted of a Red Jacket faced with blue, and worn with white Breeches. Established strength of the Corps was to be 5 Companies, each numbering 62 men, but a Letter in the Plasnewydd MSS[1] states. "We are three hundred strong and are divided into 5 Companies of sixty each."

The Officers, whose dress was also similar to their Line Infantry contemporaries but which was laced with silver, are listed as follows:

Lieut. Colonel Commandant Thomas Assheton Smith
Major David Ellis
Captain William Williams
Captain Owen Anthony Poole[2]
Captain Robert Roberts
Captain John Jones
Captain Hugh Ellis
Lieut. Zaccheus Jones
Lieut. William Roberts
Lieut. Robert Humphreys
Lieut. Owen Lloyd
Lieut. Robert Williams
Ensign William Robyns
Ensign Samuel Lloyd
Ensign William Oakes
Ensign Edward Roberts
Captain Lieutenant and Adjutant John Haslam[3]
Surgeon Thomas Jones
Quartermaster John Sharpe

In February 1804, the Loyal Carnarvon was united with Volunteer Corps of Conway and Bangor to form one large Battalion styled The Loyal Bangor, Carnarvon and Conway Infantry.

Note

The Plas Newydd MSS, Series V,[4] contains the following Letter
"From Warren Bulkeley,
Baron Hill, 11th October, 1803.
Beaumaris,

The 1000 men have thus been distributed by me

Loyal Carnarvon	300	27 Aug.03
Loyal Newborough	320	27 Aug.03
Loyal Bangor	90	15 Sept.03
Loyal Eifionydd Rifle	90	10 Sept.03
Loyal Snowdon Rangers Rifle	80	15 Sept.03
Loyal Conway	120	17 Sept.03

Thomas James Warren Bulkeley, 7th Viscount, and Lord Lieutenant of the County in this letter accounts to Government for the distribution of strength of the number of Volunteers allowed to be raised in Caernarfonshire, but the dates of acceptance given differ from dates given in later official Lists. A likely explanation is that the date given against each unit in his Letter is the date on which he, as Lord Lieutenant, approved the raising of that Corps, and not the date of official acceptance by the King.

BANGOR VOLUNTEER INFANTRY 1803-1804

Raised by John Roberts, Esq., this small Corps consisted of 1 Company of 90 Volunteers. Accepted for service by the Crown on the 7th October, 1803, they were clothed in a style similar to that worn by the Infantry of the Line.
Officers of the Corps were:
Captain John Roberts
1st Lieut. Thomas Roberts
Ensign Joseph Pring
Ensign David Pierce — all of whom received Lord Lieutenant's Commissions dated 15th September, 1803. In February, 1804, the Corps was united with the Infantry Volunteers of Caernarfon and Conway to form a new body styled Loyal Bangor, Carnarvon and Conway Infantry.

The Rules of this Corps translated from the original Welsh version appear in *Bygones* 1897/98 (267.263)

D. Hastings Irwin in his *War Medals and Decorations*, 4th Edition, 1910 describes a Medal to the Bangor Volunteers, 1805. Awarded for shooting proficency it is inscribed — 'The best shot at ball firing at 100 yards. Wm Jones made 5 hits out of 10 shots at the June firings.
An oval engraved piece.

LOYAL CONWAY INFANTRY VOLUNTEERS 1803-1804

Raised by George Thomas Smith, Esq., the Corps consisted of two Companies each numbering 60 Volunteers. Accepted for service by the Crown on 7th October, 1803, the unit was in February 1804 united with the Volunteers of Bangor and Caernarfon to form a new Corps styled 'Bangor, Carnarvon and Conway Volunteers'.

The Uniform Dress consisted of the Red Infantry Jacket with blue facing, and was worn with white breeches and the usual accoutrements.

Its Officers commissioned by the Lord Lieutenant on the 17th September, 1803, were,

Captain George Thomas Smith (Captain Commandant)
Captain Robert Hamilton
1st Lieut. William Jones
1st Lieut. Damuel Read
2nd Lieut. Edward Woodcock
2nd Lieut. Owen Roberts

LOYAL NEWBOROUGH INFANTRY VOLUNTEERS 1803-1808

Raised by Lord Newborough and with Headquarters at Glynllifon, the Corps was accepted for service by the Crown on the 7th October, 1803. Second in Command of the Corps, Major William Glynne Griffith, and other Officers received Lord Lieutenant's Commissions on the 27th August, and unit establishment was fixed as follows:

2 Field Officers, 5 Captains, 10 Subalterns, 15 Sergeants, 15 Corporals, 5 Drummers, 320 Privates, which last were organised in five Companies each numbering 64 Volunteers.

On the 4th November, 1803, a Supernumerary Company of 100 Volunteers was accepted for service with the Corps. These men, mainly tenants from the Newborough Estate, agreed to serve without pay, and were not entitled to any of the privileges granted to Volunteers generally. The running costs of this additional Company styled the Loyal Newborough Supernumerary Volunteers, was met from Lord Newborough's private purse. The Company was increased to 180 Volunteers by February 1804.

The Uniform Dress of this Corps — a Red Jacket faced with blue and worn with White Breeches was similar in most respects to that worn by the Line Infantry. Undoubtedly the best found Corps in the County due to Lord Newborough's personal involvement, the unit when on parade compared very favourably with their contemporaries in the regular service.

In October 1804, the Corps less its Light Companies which were away on permanent duty[5] in Conway, was reviewed and inspected in Caernarfon by

Major General Heron commanding the District. The General "expressed his warmest commendation of their conduct, and said he would report them fit for any service whatsoever."[6] The Officers, Non Commissioned Officers and Other Ranks were, with the exception of the Sergeant Major, all tenants of Lord Newborough.

In June 1805 the Corps marched to Conway for a period of Permanent Duty which culminated in the customary annual inspection.[7] As in the previous year the results were most satisfactory, a standard which the Corps maintained throughout its existence.

Beaumaris was the venue for the Permanent Duty of 1808, the Corps under the command of Colonel W.G. Griffiths spending 13 days in the town commencing 20th May. In June of that same year Lieut. Colonel Glynne took over command of the Corps following the death of Lord Newborough, its founder and financial benefactor.[8]

In September 1808, the Corps stood down, but a proportion of its Officers and Men voluntarily extended their services as members of the newly formed Regiment of Carnarvonshire Local Militia.

A Medal for Merit awarded to a member of the Corps exists. An oval silver piece suspended from a red ribbon edged in blue. One side is engraved with the Royal Cipher 'GR' and a Trophy of Weapons and Flags over a three part scroll inscribed 'Loyal Newborough Volunteers'.

LOYAL EIFIONYDD VOLUNTEERS 1803-1808

Raised by William Williams, Esq., the Corps was accepted for service by the Crown on the 7th October, 1803, and was in fact a revival of the earlier Corps which had stood down in the same district in 1802. Clothed in Red Jackets faced with blue and worn with light blue Breeches, the coats worn by the Officers were suitably embellished with gold lace.

The establishment was set at 1 Captain, 2 Subalterns, 4 Sergeants, 4 Corporals, 1 Drummer and 80 Private men, the whole forming one Company. The Officers commissioned on the 10th September, 1803, were:
Captain William Williams. Lieut. Griffith Thomas, Lieut. John Morris and Ensign Morris Jones.

Also referred to as the Loyal Eifionydd Rifles, Loyal Eifionydd Infantry and Eifionydd Infantry Volunteers the Corps is recorded as being present in Pwllheli for 13 days Permanent Duty in June 1808.[9] In September of that year it stood down on formation of the County Regiment of Local Militia and into which a number of its Officers and Other Ranks were voluntarily absorbed.

At Christie's Militaria Sale, May 20th, 1988, Lot 121 was suggested to be a Coatee (short tailed) of the pattern worn by Officers of this Corps, c.1803. Purchased by the Royal Welch Fusiliers Museum the scarlet cloth garment has a plain dark blue collar and blue pointed cuffs and has gold laced scarlet

MERIT MEDAL. LOYAL NEWBOROUGH INFANTRY VOLUNTEERS
c.1803. Silver. Red Ribbon with Blue edging.

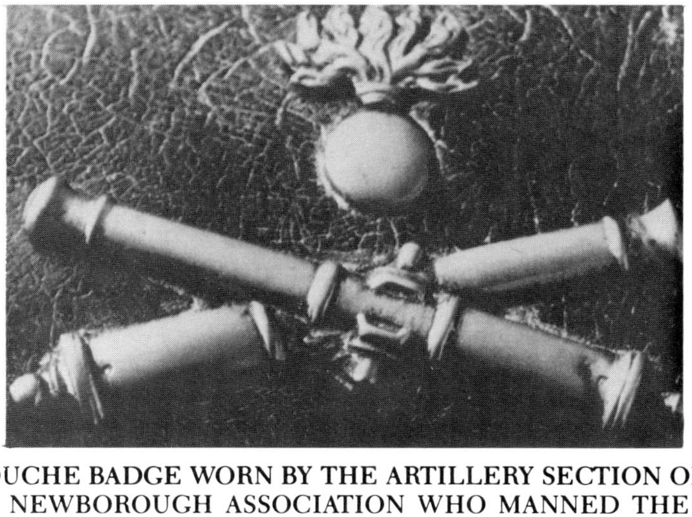

CARTOUCHE BADGE WORN BY THE ARTILLERY SECTION OF THE LOYAL NEWBOROUGH ASSOCIATION WHO MANNED THE FORT BELAN CANNON c.1800

cloth, winged epaulettes on each shoulder, both fringed with gold and bearing bugle horn ornaments. The front of the coat is embellished with two rows of equally spaced gilt buttons, convex, openbacked and bearing the letters 'L.E.V.' Similar buttons adorn each winged epaulette, the cuffs, pocket flaps and pleats on the back of the Jacket. The turnbacks of white cloth carry no distinctive badge or embellishment.

There exists also a brass oval Cross Belt Plate of the pattern worn by Other Ranks, c.1803. It carries the design of the Plumes, Coronet and Motto of the Prince of Wales with a small foliated decoration on each side of the Motto scrolls. Above the Plumes, on the upper rim of the Plate, the incorrectly spelt title 'LOYAL EFIONYDD'.

The Plate forms part of the collection of the Museum of Welsh Antiquities, University College of North Wales, Bangor.

LOYAL SNOWDEN RANGERS 1803-1808

Raised by Sir Robert Williams, Bt, of Nant, this small Corps was accepted for service by the Crown on the 7th October, 1803. Its Officers were Captain Sir Robert Williams, Bt,
Lieut. Robert Morris
and Ensign ... Jones, all of whom received Commissions dated 15th September, 1803.

The Establishment of the Corps was set at 1 Captain, 2 Subalterns, 4 Corporals, 1 Drummer and one Company of 80 Private Men. In keeping with its 'Rifles' role, the Uniform Dress worn by its members consisted of a Rifle Green Jacket faced with black, which was worn with Rifle Green Breeches and Black Leather Accoutrements.

Also referred to as the Snowdon Rangers Riflemen and Snowdon Volunteer Infantry the Loyal Snowden had its establishment of Private Men reduced to 60 on February 2nd, 1804, a move directed towards bringing the total number of voluteers active in the County closer to the authorised figure.

Like other Volunteer Corps it trained locally, except for one period ranging from 7 to 21 days annually, when it marched out to another town in the County or neighbouring county for a period of Permanent Duty. Such was the case in June 1808 when the Loyal Snowden joined the united Bangor, Caernarfon and Conway Corps for 13 days permanent duty in Beaumaris.[10] Such assemblies were generally looked forward to by the inhabitants of the town selected. For the Gentry it gave an excuse for a lively round of social events, and for the Tradespeople a sharp increase of business. During such periods, the Other Ranks of the Volunteers were billeted in such accommodation as could be provided by the Inns and Lodging Houses of the town.

In September 1808, the Loyal Snowden stood down, but a number of its members voluntarily transferred their services to the new regiment of Carnarvonshire Local Militia.

OFFICERS SCARLET COATEE WITH BLUE FACINGS.
LOYAL EIFIONYDD INFANTRY VOLUNTEERS, c.1803
By kind permission of Christies

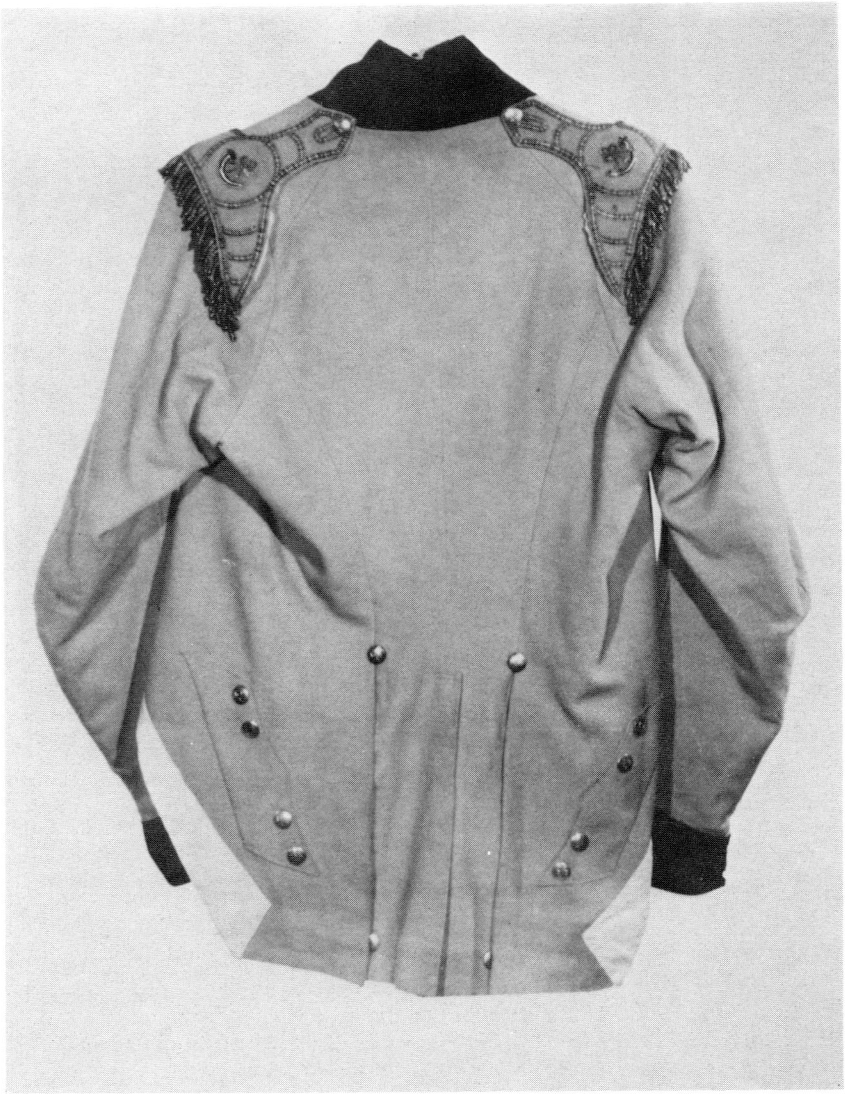

REAR VIEW
OFFICERS SCARLET COATEE WITH BLUE FACINGS
LOYAL EIFIONYDD INFANTRY VOLUNTEERS, c.1803
By kind permission of Christies

Top Centre
Cross Belt Plate, Royal Carnarvon Fusiliers Militia, c.1800

Bottom Left
Cross Belt Plate. Loyal Newborough Association Volunteers, c.1803

Bottom Right
Cross Belt Plate. Loyal Eifionydd Infantry Volunteers, c.1803

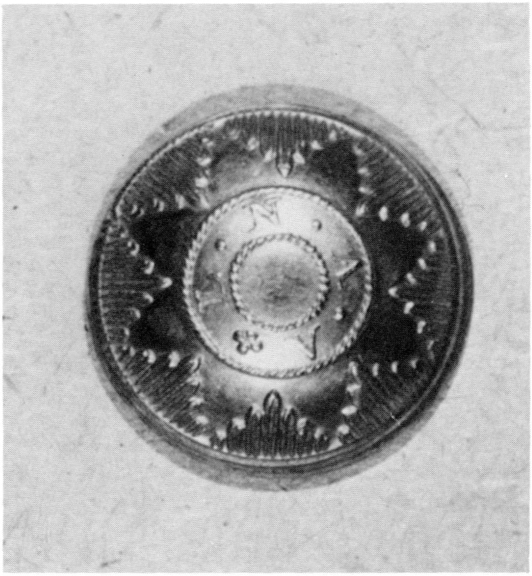

BUTTON. OFFICERS COATEE.
LOYAL NEWBOROUGH INFANTRY
VOLUNTEERS, c.1803
(Owen Collection)

LOYAL BANGOR, CARNARVON AND CONWAY INFANTRY 1804-1808

In February 1804, the hitherto independent Bangor, Caernarfon and Conway Corps of Infantry Volunteers were amalgamated to form one large Corps or Battalion under the command of Lieut. Colonel Thomas Assheton Smith of Vaynol. The Establishment set for the new organisation was 2 Field Officers, 8 Captains, 17 Subalterns, 3 Staff Officers, 25 Sergeants, 17 Corporals, 8 Drummers and 520 Private Men divided amongst 8 Companies. The Uniform Dress consisted of a Red Jacket with blue facings, worn with White Breeches, similar to the uniform then worn by the Regular Infantry of the Line.

On Wednesday, 15th August, 1804, some 450 members of the Corps assembled in Vaynol Park to receive a Stand of Colours from Mrs Assheton Smith. Later that same day, the Corps was inspected by Lieut. Colonel Knight, Inspecting Field Officer Volunteers, N.W. District, who expressed great satisfaction with their appearance and drill.[11] Sadly, the Colours do not appear to have survived, but it is likely that when the Corps stood down in 1808, that the Stand, in accordance with custom, was returned to the donor or became property of the Officer Commanding the Corps.

Beaumaris was a popular venue for annual training, the Corps mustering there for permanent duty in 1804-05-06 and 07. On each occasion they received the thanks of the townsmen for their exemplary conduct. During the 1807 training, the Inspecting Field Officer described them as "equal to any Regular Regiment in the precision of their firing and correctness of movement."[12]

On the 12th April, 1808, the Bangor Companies were inspected in that place by Lieut. Colonel Warrington, who, "took much pains in the examination of the Corps, on the termination of which he assured Captain Roberts that he approved highly of their steadiness, discipline, and soldierlike appearance."[13] Beaumaris was the venue for the year's annual training: "On Monday morning, the Volunteers of the City (Bangor) marched to Bangor Ferry where they were joined by the Carnarvon Volunteers and Snowdon Rangers commanded by Major Williams; from where they proceeded across the ferry to Beaumaris on Permanent Duty for 13 days. Their number and appearance were highly creditable to this part of the Principality."

This training period was to be the last attended by the Corps' prior to stand down and conversion to Local Militia, and prior to its departure the occasion was marked by a Grand Ball arranged by Lieut. Colonel Smith for the Gentry of Beaumaris and district. The Press recording the Corps departure from the town said "A more soldierlike and respectable Corps we never remember to have seen, and their attention, orderliness and respectful conduct are represented to us to have been highly meritorious and will long be remembered by the inhabitants of Beaumaris."[15]

Towards the end of July, the various Companies assembled at their drill stations to record the number of men prepared to transfer their services into the Carnarvonshire Regiment of Local Militia. The response of both Bangor and Caernarfon Companies was both enthusiastic and immediate.

"We have the satisfaction of stating to the Principality that on Monday last that well disciplined Corps, the Carnarvon Volunteers assembled for the purpose of considering the propriety of entering as Local Militiamen under the late Act, when after an animated explanatory address by Colonel Smith, they loyally resolved to enter into that engagement.

Last evening, with an unanimity unparalleled, the Bangor Volunteers, after an appropriate address from Major Williams, came forward to a man with the firm step of patriotism as Local Militiamen to defend their King and Country with the spirit of Ancient Britons."[16]

In September 1808, the Corps stood down, but numbers of its Officers and Men as selected continued in service under Lieut. Colonel Assheton Smith in the newly formed regiment of Carnarvonshire Local Militia.

Footnotes

1. Plasnewydd MSS. Series V. University College of North Wales, Bangor
2. See also Carnarvon Volunteer Association 17898-1802

3. Previously had served 5 years with the Shropshire Militia
4. University College of North Wales, Bangor
5. A period of paid duty/annual training
6. Cambrian 2nd November, 1804
7. Cambrian 7th June, 1805
8. North Wales Gazette 12th May and June 9th, 1808
9. North Wales Gazette 16th June, 1808
10. North Wales Gazette 16th June, 1808
11. Cambrian 5th July, 1805 and 20th October 1807
13. North Wales Gazette 14th April, 1808
14. North Wales Gazette 16th June, 1808
15. North Wales Gazette 30th June, 1808
16. North Wales Gazette 28th July, 1808

LOCAL MILITIA 1808-1816

The Local Militia Act[1] which became Law on the 30th June, 1808, swept away, with the exception of Yeomanry Cavalry, and a few Corps of Artillery and Infantry Volunteers who continued in service for a period at their own expense, a Force of Infantry Volunteers which had grown so large as to become almost unmanageable from a military point of view. Additionally, there had been tied up within the Volunteer ranks a large proportion of the nation's fittest and most useful manpower, protected from the demands of both Regular Army and the Militia by reason of their Volunteer privileges.

The formation of a more malleable force of Local Militia prompted the Historian Fortescue to write — "Two hundred thousand men who could be compelled to undergo training and to do as they were told were substituted for an uncertain number, who after great expense to the Country, still claimed the glorious privilege of doing as they pleased. The gain to the country was enormous; and as a natural consequence, a large proportion of the Regular Army was released for service beyond the sea."[2]

Not to be confused with the 'Regular or County' Militia which at that time was embodied and out of both counties on garrison duty, a Local Militiaman, whether recruited voluntarliy or selected by ballot, was required to serve for four years. No Substitutes were allowed, but certain categories of men, could, on payment of a fine of between £10 and £30, gain exemption for a period of two years. Where enforcement of the Local Militia Ballot was necessary to complete numbers, it was applied to men between the ages of 18 and 30 years, who in addition to being compelled to attend a period of annual training, could, in the event of rebellion or invasion, be marched with their regiment to any part of Great Britain. In the ordinary course of events, a Local Militiaman was not expected to serve outside the boundaries of his own or neighbouring Counties. In those districts, the Lords Lieutenant were empowered to use them in Aid of Civil Power for a period of up to 14 days. Men serving in the new Force were to be actively encouraged to enlist in the Militia and the Line, but they could not volunteer or be recruited for such service during the period selected for their annual training.

The Anglesey and Caernarvonshire Local Militia Regiments did not assemble for training in 1808 due to the fact that they had already completed the period of permanent duty required of them as Volunteers. The first assembly took place in 1809 for a period of 28 days, but, as will be seen, that was reduced to 14 days at a later date.

In July 1808, Commanding Officers of the Volunteer Corps active in both counties had received a letter from the War Office requesting them to specify the number and rank of persons serving in their Corps who were prepared to enlist voluntarily in the Local Militia.[3]

The response in both counties was favourable, and with the exception of Caernarfonshire where 12 men had to be selected by ballot, the number of Local Militiamen required which amounted to six times the quota set for the Regular Militia of both counties was met by voluntary enlistment.

To begin with, service with the new regiments appeared to be little different to that rendered in Volunteer Corps, but as time progressed it became less popular. The men missed the compactness and conviviality of the old Volunteer Corps and the regulations governing their new activities made them feel more like 'pressed men'. In consequence, few could be persuaded to re-engage on completion of their four year stint in 1812; thereafter, the numbers required were drawn almost entirely by ballot. Even Commanding Officers felt need to complain when in December 1809 they found themselves required to insure Arms, Clothing and other stores placed in their charge, as a letter circulated to them during that month made it clear that in the event of loss through cause other than embodied service, they would be personally responsible to Government for its value.[4]

In comparison to the Local Militia of other counties in England and Wales the regiments of Anglesey and Carnarvonshire had a comparatively trouble free existence, and were not plagued by overmuch desertion, disputes, and occasional near mutiny over the payment of certain allowances. Fortescue opines that the Government soon found the Local Militia to be more costly to maintain than it had anticipated: furthermore, the Force was not providing the numbers expected for service with the Line and Militia. The military value of the Local Militia was also being questioned as their total training time per annum amounted to less than had been put in by their Volunteer predecessors.

In pursuit of economy, the Government reduced Permanent Staff, and in March 1811, the number of days training (with the exception of recruits) was reduced to 14 days per annum.

In 1813, an Act allowed Local Militia to volunteer, should the need arise, for garrison duty outside their regimental boundaries. Both Anglesey and Carnarvonshire Regiments expressed willingness to undertake such service.

The Local Militia continued to be trained up to 1815, but in May 1816 an Act[5] suspending the Local Militia Ballot was passed and enrolment for the Force then ceased. By the end of that year the various regiments had stood down or were in the process of doing so, and the Force passed on into the pages of history.

Footnotes

1. 48 Geo III. c.3
2. Fortescue. J.W. History of the British Army. Vol IV. p.183
3. Cambrian. 22nd July, 1808
4. Cambrian. 15th December, 1809
5. 56. Geo III. c.38

ANGLESEY LOCAL MILITIA 1809-1816

No Return has been found which gives the exact number of Volunteers from the Anglesey Companies who voluntarily transferred their services into the County Regiment of Local Militia, which regiment, unlike that of Caernarfonshire, does not appear to have got off the ground until January 1809. Like the Volunteers whom they had succeeded, Local Militiamen were obliged to complete a number of days training in every year, but unlike their predecessors, were confined in the first instance to 28 days of permanent duty.

In 1809 the Anglesey Local Militia assembled in Beaumaris in June where they are reported to have conducted themselves with "distinguished credit." Prior to dismissing the regiment the men in the ranks were treated by Lord Bulkeley to an excellent dinner and a "liberal allowance of cwrw da".[1]

In June 1810, the regiment trained in Beaumaris for 20 days and was inspected on the 23rd of the month by General Montresser who was pleased to "pass the most deserved eulogies" upon the Corps.[2]

In November of the same year, at a ceremony held in that town, Major Sir Robert Williams (late the Snowdon Rangers) acting in the name of the Officers of the regiment presented Colonel The Rt. Hon. Lord Bulkeley with a Sword in appreciation of his services to the county and the regiment. During the ceremony Beaumaris was bedecked with Flags and Bunting, and a Salute was fired from the Beaumaris Battery and returned by the Armed Vessels then lying in the Harbour. The day of festivity and ceremonial was rounded off by a Dinner for the Officers at Barham Hill, and his Lordship arranged similar for the Non-Commissioned Officers of the regiment at the Bulls Head Inn.[3]

The Regiment assembled in like fashion at Beaumaris annually and in 1813 was one of the Local Militia Corps which volunteered to serve the Crown in any part of the country should such need arise.[4] It last assembled in 1815 and then stood down during the general disembodiment which followed the ending of hostilities.

Footnotes

1. Cambrian. 7th July, 1809. N. Wales Gazette. 29th June, 1809
2. Cambrian. 29th June, 1810. N.Wales Gazette. 21st June, 1810
3. Cambrian. November 9th, 1810

   Cambrian. December 24th, 1813

UNIFORM DRESS

The Uniform Dress worn by the Anglesey Local Militia was similar to that worn by Line Infantry of the day and is briefly described in official lists as Red with Blue Facings.

No example of the Uniform Jacket worn by Officers or Other Ranks has, as far as is known, survived to the present day.

COLOURS

Unlike their Volunteer predecessors, the regiments of Local Militia received a Stand of Colours from Government sources in the same manner as the County Militia. No record has been found to date describing the presentation of Colours, but the ceremony very likely took place in Beaumaris during the 1809 training.

Sometime in 1816, or shortly thereafter, the Colours together with the Arms of the regiment were returned to the Tower of London, and there remained until 1913, when a number of those which were still in reasonable condition were handed back into the care of the appropriate County authority. As far as is known, the Colours of the Anglesey Local Militia did not survive to be returned to Beaumaris.

BADGES AND BUTTONS

The Officers Shoulder Belt Plate consisted of an oblong gilt plate with rounded corners. Superimposed at the centre, an oval belt and Crown. The belt is inscribed with the Motto 'PRO ARIS ET FOCIS', the whole gilded. Inside the belt on a plain gilded ground, the Plumes, Coronet and Motto of the Prince of Wales, the Coronet Gilded and the Plumes and Motto Scrolls, silver. Below this central device, the engraved letters 'R.A.L.M.'

No explanation for the inclusion 'Royal' in the regimental title has been found, but similar and likely unofficial examples of such usage may be found in both Cardiganshire and Carmarthenshire.

SHOULDER BELT PLATE.
ANGLESEY LOCAL MILITIA, 1808-16

PLATE. CROSS BELT. ANGLESEY LOCAL MILITIA, 1808-16

The Cross Belt Plate depicted is drawn from a description supplied to the Author by a Collector of some standing many years ago. The confusing part of the plate is the title section R.A.L.M., as the Anglesey Local Militia was not as far as it is known entitled to use the prefix 'Royal'. The plate was described as being gilded with Silvered Plumes, Coronet and Motto.

Ref: The late H. Thomas of Swansea

Drawing by Richard Scollins.

(HEAD-QUARTERS—BEAUMARIS.)

Colonel - -	Tho. Ja. *Visc.* Bulkeley	26Jan.1809	
Lieut. Colonel	O. P. Meyrick	26Jan.1809	
Major -	*Sir* Rob. Williams, *Bt.*	26Jan.1809	
	John B. Sparrow	12Apr.	
Captain -	John Williams	26Jan.1809	
	William Sparrow	do.	
	Augustus E. Fuller	do.	
	Sir W. B. Hughes	do.	
	John Price	do.	
	J. Jackson	do.	
	R. T. Griffith	do.	
	John Jones	do.	
	Jones Panton	8Feb.1810	
	Joseph Goddard	17Mar.	
Lieutenant	William Williams	26Jan.1809	
	Owen Roberts	do.	
	William Price	do.	
	Griffith Roberts	do.	
	John Jones	do.	
	W. Hughes	do.	
	W. Thomas	do.	
	Henry Hughes	do.	
	James Williams	do.	
	James Webster	do.	
	John Evans	do.	
	Robert Pritchard	do.	
	John Paynter	do.	Supernumerary
	John Owen	do.	Do.
	W. Williams	do.	Do.
	Thomas Lewis	do.	Do.
	William Owen	do.	Do.
	Peter Webster	do.	Do.
Ensign -	John Lloyd	29Jan.1809	
	Richard Lewis	do.	
	James Fisher	do.	
	Hugh Williams	do.	
	Henry Price	19May	
	John Griffith	do.	
	James Harris	21May1811	
	William Hughes	7June	
Adjutant	John Jones		Captain
	Theoph. Jones		Supernumerary
Quarter-Mr.	Richard Lewis	26Jan.1809	
	John Parry	do.	Supernumerary
Surgeon -	Griffith Roberts	26Jan.1809	

ANGLESEY LOCAL MILITIA
(Militia List 1810)

CARNARVONSHIRE LOCAL MILITIA 1808-1816

Officially formed in September 1808, the Officers and Men appear mainly to have been drawn from Lieut. Colonel Thomas Assheton Smith's consolidated Corps of Bangor, Caernarfon and Conway Volunteers who as previously mentioned volunteered en masse. The regiment assembled for its first annual training at Caernarfon in June 1809 and was present there for 28 days. The Inspecting Field Officer on that occasion stated that the regiment "performed with distinguished credit" and complimented them on their regularity and steadiness in the Field.[1] The Clothing Allowance for the regiment which assembled only once in every year is of interest: Sergeant Major, £4.10s per annum, Sergeants £3.10s, Drum Major £4.1s.9d, Corporals, £2, Drummers £3.1s.9d., Private Men £1.19s.6d.[2]

In June 1810, the Regiment trained again in Caernarfon, on which occasion they were inspected by Brigadier General Montressor on the 22nd of the month. As in the previous year, the regiment was complimented on its performance during training and inspection.[3]

In 1811 the regiment trained only for 14 days which period ended on June 2nd. The press reporting the annual inspection stated, "We feel highly gratified in paying our tribute of praise and admiration as to their exemplary conduct in Quarters,[4] and their high state of discipline[5] in the Field, which have received the most marked acknowledgement from the Inspecting Officer of the District, General Gamel."[6]

Caernarfon provided the venue for the 1812, 1813, 1814 and 1815 assemblies, the press reporting the 1813 inspection as follows: "The Carnarvonshire Local Militia commanded by Colonel Smith were inspected on Saturday by Major General Laird. The regiment went through several manoeuvres with a precision which would have done credit to an old established Corps; and drew from the General, the well deserved mead of unqualified approbation, and he promised that he would make a particular report of the soldierlike conduct of the regiment."[7]

During the same year the Caernarfonshire Corps was one of the Local Militia Regiments who volunteered for Garrison Duty in any part of the country as and when required. No such call was made upon them, and in 1815 its short chapter in the County military history was finally closed.

Footnotes

1. Cambrian. 7th July, 1809. N. Wales Gazette 29th June, 1809
2. N.Wales Gazette. January 16th, 1809
3. N.Wales Gazette. June 21st, 1810
4. During training the men were billeted on public houses and lodging houses about the town
5. The word 'discipline' in this context refers to their expertise at Foot Drill and Drill under Arms.
6. Cambrian. June 1811
7. Cambrian. July 2nd, 1813

UNIFORM DRESS

The Uniform Dress worn by the regiment is described as Red, Facings, Blue. It was similar to that worn by similar ranks of the Line Infantry of the period. As far as is known, not one piece has survived through to the present day.

COLOURS

A Stand of Colours was issued by Ordnance to the regiment, but no record of the date or description of the ceremony has been found. The Carnarvonshire Local Militia Colours do not appear to have survived to be returned to the County in 1913.

BADGES AND BUTTONS

A Cross Belt Plate of the pattern worn by the Carnarvonshire Local Militia was many years ago presented to The Welsh Folk Museum by the Misses Isambard Owen. Listed under Accession No.51.411/170 the plate, for which no description exists, was later misplaced or stolen when on loan to a North Wales Museum and has not since been recovered.

CARNARVONSHIRE YEOMANRY CAVALRY

In 1819, as in 1795, yet another attempt was made to raise a Corps of Yeomanry Cavalry in the County, the prime mover on this occasion being one Captain H.P. Griffith.

Benson Freeman, R.N.R., in No. 38 of his series of Articles on the *Historical Records of the Yeomanry Regiments*[1] includes a letter dated 12th November, 1819, in which Lord Sidmouth informs Captains Griffith of the procedure for raising, and of the Government Allowances made to such Corps.

As in 1795, the matter appears to have progressed no further than the discussion stage, and no record has been found in the Official Lists to support the existence of a Carnarvonshire Corps.

Footnote

Territorial Services Gazette

(HEAD-QUARTERS—CARNARVON.)

Lt. Col. Com.	Tho. Assheton Smith	24Sept.1808	
Lieut. Colonel	W. Williams	19May1809	
Major - -	John Ellis	30Aug.1810	
Captain -	Robert Roberts	24Sept.1808	
	John Jones	do.	
	John Roberts	do.	
	Robert Beaver	do.	
	E. G. Roberts	19May1809	
	Sir R. Williams, *Bt.*	11July	
	Thomas Jones	do.	
	William Roberts	13June1810	
	Robert Humphreys	7June1811	
	.		
Lieutenant	John Hughes	24Sept.1808	
	W. Oakes	do.	
	W. Parry	24Oct.	
	Robert Williams	19May1809	
	T. H. Jones	do.	
	Thomas Payne	do.	
	Robert Jones	do.	
	D. R. Pughe	do.	
	Richard Jones	do.	
	W. Owen	13June1810	
	W. Owen	do.	
	Evan Evans	7June1811	
Ensign -	Edward Edwarts	19May1809	
	John Griffith	7June1811	
	.		
	.		
	.		
Adjutant	J. Haslam	24Sept.1808	
	David Griffith	do.	Supernumerary
Quarter-Mast.	Owen Pritchard	24Oct.1808	
Surgeon -	Thomas Jones	24Sept.1808	
	R. Curry	24Oct.	Supernumerary

CARNARFONSHIRE LOCAL MILITIA
(Militia List 1810)

ROYAL NAVAL ARTILLERY VOLUNTEERS

THE CARNARVON ROYAL NAVY ARTILLERY VOLUNTEERS

The presence in 1881 of a Battery of Royal Naval Volunteers in Carnarfon town suggest that they may well have emerged from a predecessor Corps known as the Royal Naval Coast Volunteers which had come into existence nationally in the year 1852. Drawn from the seafaring community, the members of the R.N.C.V. contracted to serve afloat up to a limit of 150 miles offshore should the need arise, but their primary role was coastal defence — their training in such matters being until 1856 the responsibility of the Coast Guard Service.

Men enlisted for a five year period, and received 65 shillings pay per annum provided they successfully completed in each year a 28 day training period. Additionally, such service exempted them from any compulsory service with the Royal Navy. In 1856, control of the force passed into the hands of the Board of Admiralty, several of whose members were opposed to the principles on which the R.N.C.V. was formed. They felt that something stronger and more closely linked to the regular service was required. Hence in 1859, the Royal Naval Reserve was formed, whose close links with the Royal Navy and more attractive terms of service resulted in a weakening in numbers and a falling off in the popularity of the older service.

The R.N.C.V. did not really get off the ground in Wales until 1856 when Captain J.V. Baker, R.N., was appointed to organise the movement in the Principality. It is likely that somewhere between that date and 1872, a detachment of R.N.C.V. came into existence in Caernarfon although no record of its raising has to date been found by this writer.

Due to competition from the R.N.R., the R.N.C.V. had by 1872 been reduced nationally to less than 1000 Volunteers, which survivors were in that same year renamed Royal Naval Artillery Volunteers. The accompanying photographs show what appears to be a thriving detachment in Carnarvon town in the 1880s where, in addition to Cutters supplied for small boat training, the Volunteer must have had access to Coast Artillery pieces on which to carry out their Gunnery practice.

The R.N.A.V. continued to serve in ever weakening numbers until absorbed by the R.N.R. and R.N.R. Volunteers in the mid 1880s. The last record found of their presence is in an account of a ceremony for the presentation of new Colours to the 4th (Militia) Battalion, Royal Welsh Fusiliers in May 1885 when the Carnarvon Battery under the command of Lieut. C.A. Jones, R.N.A.V., kept the ground and consisted of Officers and Men of the Battery who attended the Windsor Volunteer Review of 1881.

CARNARVON ROYAL NAVAL ARTILLERY VOLUNTEERS. c.1881

Included in the Photograph are the following local personalities

Robert Jones, William Williams Jim Clayton Williams, A.W. Roberts, J. Edwards, R. Hope, J. Roberts, D. Francis, R.R. Williams, Noble, W.W. Thomas, J. Litherland, James, Bill Jones, John Williams, D.T. Edwards, J. Jones, B. Jones, Jack Jones, Tom Harwood, Tom Richards, Williams Owen, O. Evans, J. Pugh, J. Jones (2), J.G. Jones, G. Humphries, B. Pritchard, Hugh Jenkins, R. Parry, George Owen.

By kind permission of the Gwynedd Archives Service (Caernarfon Office)

CARNARVON ROYAL NAVAL ARTILLERY VOLUNTEERS. JUBILEE YEAR. 1887
By kind permission of Gwynedd Archives Service (Caernarfon Office)

CARNARVONSHIRE ARTILLERY VOLUNTEERS. JUBILEE YEAR. 1887
By kind permission of Gwynedd Archives Service (Caernarfon Office)

VOLUNTEERS 1859-1908

The forty years which followed the final defeat of Napoleonic France at Waterloo, were from the point of view of home defence, decades of very much reduced military activity. With the Militia disembodied, and machinery for re-activating Local Militia suspended, the public was only occasionally reminded of the existence of non-Regular Troops, by the appearance in certain districts of Yeomanry Cavalry Corps on exercise, reviews, or duties in connection with their role in Aid of Civil Power. By the mid 1840s concern was being expressed about the inadequacy of the nation's defences. Even the great Duke of Wellington was unhappy with the situation, and expressed his concern in 1847 in a letter to Sir John Burgoyne, Inspector General of Fortifications.

A step in the right direction, was the revival of the Militia a few years before the outbreak of the War in the Crimea — a campaign in which the ancient adversary, France, fought alongside Great Britain as an ally. The War exposed the shortcomings of the British Army organisation which followed by the pressure put upon it during the Indian Mutiny crisis, caused fears to be expressed as to its ability to cope properly with both demands of Empire and defence of our island shore. The growing influence of Napoleon III and an expansion of French Naval Power caused even more concern, but proposals to recreate the Volunteer Force found little favour with the Government of the day.

Matters came to a head in 1858 when after an attempt on the life of the French Emperor, it was disclosed that the Italian assassin had plotten murder and prepared his bomb on British soil. In France, outraged French militarists clamoured for revenge: so much so, that their persistent threats and sabre rattling was interpreted by the British public as nothing less than a threat to invade. The upshot was a wave of patriotic fervour throughout the land, the result of which in due course forced the Government to give way to sanction a revival of the Volunteer movement.

The Yeomanry and Volunteer Consolidation Act of 1804 had consolidated or amended as necessary all previous legislation appertaining to such units, and being unrepealed, conveniently provided the constitutional means for a re-creation of the Force. On May 12th, 1859, the Secretary for War sent out to the Lords Lieutenant a Circular announcing the Queen's approval of a measure to permit the raising of Volunteer Corps under the provisions of the 1804 Act.

The intensity of the response surprised both Government and the Military: no less than 161 Rifle Corps receiving recognition before the end of the year. In addition Corps of Artillery and Engineer Volunteers were also raised, thus laying the foundations for a large Citizen Soldier Force. Those men who came forward in their thousands in 1859/60 were to be the foreunners of the later Territorial Force and of the present smaller, but highly efficient Territorial Army.

THE ARTILLERY VOLUNTEERS 1860-1878
ANGLESEY

ANGLESEY ARTILLERY VOLUNTEERS

The Volunteer Revival of 1859/60 saw three Artillery Volunteer Corps raised in the County of Anglesey.

1st Corps (Holyhead)
Raised: December 1860

Captain John Jacobs	14th December, 1860

2nd Corps (Holyhead)
Raised: December 1860

Captain Charles Rigby	14th December, 1860

3rd Corps (Beaumaris)
Raised: December 1860

Captain William H. Weldon	14th December, 1860
1st Lieut. Richard Williams	19th December, 1860
2nd Lieut. Owen Owen, Jnr.	19th December, 1860

The Army List for May/August 1862 shows some changes

1st Corps (Holyhead)

Captain Hon. W. Owen Stanley	7.3.1861
1st Lieut. William Lloyd Hughes	7.3.1861
2nd Lieut. Edward Benjamin Cunnah	7.3.1861
Hon. A/Surgeon John Richard Price	24.7.1861

2nd Corps (Holyhead)

Captain Charles Rigby	14.12.1860
1st Lieut. Robert Leech Cousins	26.12.1860
2nd Lieut. Edmund Privilegio	22.11.1861
Hon. Chaplain Rev. Thomas Briscoe	17.5.1861

3rd Corps (Beaumaris)

Captain William H. Weldon (late 18th Hussars)	14.12.1860
1st Lieut. Richard Williams	19.12.1860
2nd Lieut. John W. Jones	12.10.1861
Hon. A/Surgeon David W. Williams, M.D.,	12.10.1861
Hon. Chaplain R.E. Priestly, B.A.	12.10.1861

In August 1863, the Anglesey Artillery Volunteer Corps and the 1st Carnarvonshire Artillery Volunteer Corps (Caernarfon) were united to form the 1st Administrative Brigade, Anglesey Artillery Volunteers with Headquarters at Holyhead. Shortly thereafter, an Adjutant was appointed and the Brigade were able to enjoy the benefit of a standard form of training.

The Army List of April 1864 shows Major Hon. William Owen Stanley (26th August, 1863) in command of the Administrative Brigade, with John H. Hall, appointed 24th September, 1863, as his Adjutant. Commanding the 1st (Holyhead) Corps was Captain James Sparrow (18th November, 1863) whilst its other Officers remained unchanged.

The 2nd (Holyhead) Corps had an additional 2nd Lieutenant, namely Emilius R. Nicholson appointed 8th November, 1862, otherwise there were no other changes.

During 1868, a falling off of interest in the 2nd Corps led to its disbandment and removal from the Army List by July.

In November 1869, the Anglesey Corps of the Brigade still under the command of Major Hon. W.O. Stanley are shown as follows:

1st (Holyhead) Corps

Captain Thomas P. Elliott	29.5.1867
1st Lieut. John L. Griffith	10.6.1868
2nd Lieut. George Graves	20.4.1868
Hon. Chaplain Rev. W. Owen Jones, B.A.	2.1.1865

3rd (Beaumaris) Corps

Captain William Henry Weldon	19.3.1867
and presumably the son of the previous Captain.	
1st Lieut. John Williams	21.10.1865
2nd Lieut. William Evans	20.3.1869
Hon. A/Surgeon David W. Williams, M.D.	12.10.1861
Hon. Chaplain Rev. R.E. Priestly, B.A.	12.10.1861

Thomas P. Elliott is also listed as Hon. Quartermaster on the Administrative Brigade Staff with seniority 20th July, 1864. By April 1873 the 1st (Holyhead) Corps shows only one Officer other than the Hon. Chaplain, namely 1st Lieutenant John L. Griffiths, and the 3rd (Beaumaris) Corps still with its full complement:

3rd (Beaumaris) Corps

Captain William Evans	16.1.1871
1st Lieut. Evan R. Thomas	16.1.1871
2nd Lieut. Edwin Whittaker	16.1.1871
Hon. A/Surgeon Robert E. Owen	16.1.1871
Hon. Chaplain Rev. David Thomas, B.A.	16.1.1871

The fact that the Brigade contained only three Corps was somewhat problematical, but the matter was solved before the end of 1873 by uniting both Anglesey and Carnarvon Artillery Volunteers with the Artillery Volunteers of Cheshire which brought them under the care of the 1st Administrative Brigade Cheshire Artillery Volunteers.

1875, saw the disappearance of the 1st (Holyhead) Corps due mainly to lack of support and interest. There remained now only the Beaumaris Corps which was also suffering similar problems, indeed, by 1878 most of its members were Carnarvonshire men from Bangor and District. In consequence of this, it was decided that Anglesey could no longer support Artillery Volunteers, and by November of that year the 3rd (Beaumaris) Corps had been redesignated as the 2nd Corps Carnarvonshire Artillery Volunteers.

Return of Strength 1871

Maximum Establishment — 164
Total Enrolled — 207
Number Efficient — 199
Number Non-efficient — 8

ANGLESEY ARTILLERY VOLUNTEERS

(56)

1st CORPS (HOLYHEAD)
formed 14.12.1860

2nd CORPS (HOLYHEAD)
formed 14.12.1860

3rd CORPS (BEAUMARIS)
formed 14.12.1860

1st ADMINISTRATIVE BRIDGE
ANGLESEY ARTILLERY VOLUNTEERS
formed August 1863

1st Corps (Holyhead)
2nd Corps (Holyhead)
3rd Corps (Beaumaris)
1st Carnarvonshire Art. Vols.

July 1868
2nd (CORPS) HOLYHEAD
disbanded

1873

1st and 3rd Anglesey Corps
1st Carnarvonshire Corps

included in the

1st ADMINISTRATIVE BRIGADE
CHESHIRE ARTILLERY VOLUNTEERS

1875
1st (HOLYHEAD) CORPS
disbanded

November 1878

3rd (BEAUMARIS) CORPS, ANGLESEY ART VOLS
re-designated as
2nd CARNARVONSHIRE ARTILLERY VOLUNTEERS

ARTILLERY VOLUNTEERS 1862-1908
CAERNARVONSHIRE

CAERNARVONSHIRE ARTILLERY VOLUNTEERS (59)

Although Volunteer Artillery Corps had been raised in Anglesey in 1860, Caernarfonshire did not follow suit until 1862, when through the efforts of William Hayward, a Corps was raised on the 12th March in Carnarvon. The Army List for May 1862 gives the following information

1st (Carnarvon) Corps

Captain William Hayward	12 March, 1862
1st Lieut. William Turner	12 March, 1862

In 1863, the Carnarvon Corps was united with the 1st Administrative Brigade, Anglesey Artillery Volunteers, which resulted in the Corps receiving the services of an Adjutant, and resulting higher efficiency. On the 13th August, 1864, William Turner suceeded William Hayward as Captain of the Corps, and was by 1865 the only Officer listed. That situation remained unchanged over several years.

In 1873, the Anglesey Administrative Brigade ceased to exist, and the Carnarvon Corps and Beaumaris Corps were united with the 1st Administrative Brigade, Cheshire Artillery Volunteers. In November of that year also, the 3rd Anglesey or Beaumaris Corps, sole survivor of the three Artillery Volunteer Corps once active in that County, was renamed 2nd Carnarvon Corps and its drill station established in Bangor, the city and district most of its members were drawn from.

By June 1880, the Cheshire Administrative Brigade had been consolidated and redesignated 1st Cheshire and Carnarvonshire Artillery Volunteer Corps, an organisation of 8 Batteries of which Carnarvonshire provided No. 6 and 7 (late 2nd Carnarvonshire or Bangor Corps), and No. 8 Battery, late (1st Carnarvonshire or Carnarvon Corps). Headquarters of the new unit was located at Chester, but the Carnarvonshire Volunteer Gunners saw little of their Cheshire counterparts except for a short period of combined annual training. Precedence Number of the 1st Cheshire and Carnarvonshire in the Volunteer Artillery List was 28.

The Army List of August 1882 shows the 1st Cheshire and Carnarvonshire A.V. as forming part of the Lancashire Brigade, Royal Artillery, and by August 1889 part of the Southern Division, R.A.

By July 1904, the Carnarvonshire element of the unit was separated from that of Cheshire and reformed in its own County as the 1st CARNARVONSHIRE ARTILLERY VOLUNTEERS with Headquarters at Bangor and a precedence number 64 in the list of Royal Garrison Artillery Volunteers.

In February 1908, the following Officers are listed:

Lieut. Colonel H. Savage	5.5.1906
Captain W.C. Whiskin, V.D.	6.5.1893
Captain F. Bloom, V.D.	18.11.1896
Captain J. Samuels, V.D.	4.2.1899
Captain Sir H.R. Reichel, Kt.	18.4.1900
Lieut. R.E. Owen	18.4.1896
Lieut. W.O. Clarke	9.9.1896
Lieut. W.H. Hughes	18.11.1896
Lieut. W.H. Savage	11.7.1907
Surgeon Lieut. Colonel E.J. Lloyd, M.D., V.D.	19.10.1901 M.O.
Surgeon Lieut. C.W. Owen	9.9.1903
Rev. J.C. Morice	8.3.1905 A/Chaplain

With the formation of the Territorial Army in April 1908 the unit transferred into the Territorial Force as the WELSH (CARNARVONSHIRE) ROYAL GARRISON ARTILLERY (HEAVY), its Headquarters still at Bangor, but reduced in strength to 1 Battery.

In 1871 the total number of Artillery Volunteers enrolled in the County was 51. This had increased to 218 in 1880 and stood at 318 in 1907.

MUSTER ROLL OF EFFECTIVES
1st CARNARVON COMPANY OF ARTILLERY VOLUNTEERS — AUGUST 1862

NAME	DATE ENROLLED
Bracegirdle, William	21st March, 1862
Davies, David	21st March, 1862
Davies, Edward	21st March, 1862
Davies, John Thomas	4th July, 1862
Ensor, George Henry	21st March, 1862
Foulkes, John	21st March, 1862
Foulkes, William	21st March, 1862
Gibson, John	13th May, 1862
Griffith, William	21st March, 1862
Hughes, Lewis	21st March, 1862
Hughes, Thomas	21st March, 1862
Jones, John	21st March, 1862
Jones, Robert William	21st March, 1862
Jones, William	21st March, 1862
Jones, John	1st May, 1862
Jarrett, Edward	21st March, 1862
Jones, John	3rd June, 1862
Jones, Peter	3rd June, 1862
Jones, Owen	3rd June, 1862
Morris, Owen	21st March, 1862
Owen, John	2nd April, 1862
Owen, Richard	21st March, 1862
Owen, James Robert	21st March, 1862
Owen, Robert Humphrey	21st March, 1862
Roger, David	1st May, 1862
Parry, John Henry	21st March, 1862
Paynter, James Roose	21st March, 1862
Price, Edwin	21st March, 1862
Roberts, Thomas	21st March, 1862
Rowlands, Richard	21st March, 1862
Roberts, John	21st March, 1862
Roberts, Owen Owens	21st March, 1862
Roberts, Richard Ellis	21st March, 1862
Roberts, Robert	21st March, 1862
Rowlands, Robert Thomas	21st March, 1862
Sundival, James	21st March, 1862
Thomas, Howel	21st March, 1862

Thomas, Richard	21st March, 1862
Thomas, Elias	3rd June, 1862
Williams, William	21st March, 1862
Williams, Robert	21st March, 1862
Williams, George Henry Rumsey	21st March, 1862
Williams, Thomas Williams	26th March, 1862
Williams, Edward	21st March, 1862
Williams, John	21st March, 1862
Williams, Robert	21st March, 1862
Williams, Thomas	21st March, 1862
Jones, Richard Lloyd	21st March, 1862
Hayward, William	21st March, 1862
Turner, Williams	21st March, 1862

The men listed are all drawn from Carnarvon Parish.
The Return is submitted on W.O. Form 1613 and submitted by Captain Hayward.
Porthmadoc MSS/678 — National Library of Wales.

WELSH (CARNARVONSHIRE) ROYAL GARRISON ARTILLERY T.F.

1st CORPS (CARNARVON)
CARNARVONSHIRE ARTILLERY VOLUNTEERS
formed 12.3.1862

1st ADMINISTRATIVE BRIGADE
ANGLESEY ARTILLERY VOLUNTEERS
consisting of 3 Anglesey Corps
and 1st CARNARVONSHIRE CORPS as
from August 1863.

1873
1st CARNARVONSHIRE CORPS
included with 1st and 3rd
Anglesey Corps in the
1st ADMINISTRATIVE BRIGADE
CHESHIRE ARTILLERY VOLUNTEERS

November 1878
3rd Anglesey Corps redesignated
2nd CARNARVONSHIRE ART VOLUNTEERS
and included in the Cheshire Brigade

1880
1st ADMIN. BDE., CHESHIRE ART. VOLS.
consolidated to form
1st (CHESHIRE AND CARNARVONSHIRE) ART. VOL. CORPS
No.6 Bty. provided by 2nd Carnarvonshire Corps
No.7 Bty. provided by 2nd Carnarvonshire Corps
No.8 Battery provided by 1st Carnarvonshire Corps

July 1904
1st CARNARVONSHIRE ARTILLERY VOL. CORPS
formed from
No. 6, 7 and 8 Carnarvonshire Batteries of
the Cheshire Art. Vol. Corps.

April 1908
1st CARNARVONSHIRE R.G.A. VOLUNTEERS
transferred to the T.F.
as the
WELSH (CARNARVONSHIRE) ROYAL GARRISON
ARTILLERY (T.F.)

ANGLESEY ARTILLERY VOLUNTEERS.
CARNARVONSHIRE ARTILLERY VOLUNTEERS
UNIFORM, BADGES AND INSIGNIA

In the absence of photographs and documentary evidence it must be assumed that both Anglesey and Carnarvonshire Corps on formation wore the Uniform Dress recommended by Government in January 1860 for Corps of Artillery Volunteers. This consisted of a blue cloth jacket and trousers piped in scarlet with which was worn, in black or whitened buff leather, a belt and bayonet frog. Buttons were of silver or white metal depending on rank, and embellishment to the jacket, if any, was confined to a simple Austrian knot on each cuff. The Head-dress was likely a Forage Cap of the Pill Box pattern, or alternatively, a blue cloth Shako, low crowned, and similar to that worn by the Infantry of the Line. On the head-dress, a simple silver or white metal grenade approximately one and three quarter inches high — a badge much favoured by Volunteer Gunners. In some units, both patterns of head-dress were worn, the former for everyday wear, and the last for full dress and ceremonial occasions.

The Volunteer Regulations of 1863 directed that all Administrative Brigades and Battalions should be dressed alike, and by that date, or shortly thereafter most Artillery Volunteer Corps had adopted the basic blue uniform pattern of the Royal Artillery. No gold lace was worn by Volunteers, they, mostly from the date of formation, confining themselves to silver lace and distinctions for Officers and white metal badges and buttons for Other Ranks. In some Corps a distinctive plate was worn on the Pouch Belt, but no evidence of such has been found for either Anglesey or the Carnarvonshire Corps.

In 1878, Regulations directed the method by which the Volunteers would be distinguished from the Regulars and Militia in matters of Uniform Dress. The Artillery Volunteers were directed to wear scarlet Austrian Knots on the sleeves of their jackets and scarlet bands on their Forage Caps. The Regulars were to wear Yellow and the Militia, White. Buttons and Badges for the Artillery Volunteers remained as before, Silver or White Metal. The Anglesey Corps having disbanded in that year were not affected, but the Carnarvonshire Corps undoubtedly conformed. By that date the ceremonial/full dress head-dress worn by most Artillery Volunteer Corps was the Busby, similar in pattern to that worn by the Royal Artillery and with silver/white metal grenade plume holder. By 1880 most Corps had adopted the Home Service Pattern Blue Cloth Helmet with ball top ornament. That this was the case in Caernarfonshire a few years later, is confirmed by Lieut. Colonel Savage's photograph which is included amongst the accompanying illustrations. In the black and white photograph, Colonel Savage is dressed as would a similar ranking regular Artillery Officer of his day, but the lace and embellishments on his uniform are silver, with the exception of the rank badges on the shoulder cords and grenade collar badges, both worked in gold. A close inspection of his silver helmet plate would also identify his Corps.

CARNARVON ARTILLERY VOLUNTEER GROUP-CARNARVON CASTLE c.1870

By kind permission of the Gwynedd Archives Service

In 1902 Universal Khaki Service Dress was introduced for wear by the Army on most occasions other than ceremonial. By 1906 most Volunteer Corps were thus clothed and so remained through to their conversion into Territorial Force units in April 1908.

Examples of standard and distinctive Head-dress Badges and other Insignia are included amongst illustrations which accompany the text.

The photograph (p.143) shows a group consisting of one Officer, one Bandsman and nine other ranks with what appears to be a 32 pdr Cannon on a wrought iron garrison standing carriage. The nine Other Ranks are dressed as follows:

Head-dress

A black sealskin Busby with red cloth bag hung on the right side. On the left side, a white metal Grenade plume holder with white hair plume. The Busby measured 7.75″ at the front and 9″ at the back, It had a black leather chin strap and was lined with black cotton cloth.

Uniform

The men are wearing Tunics of blue cloth — some with red collar edged all round with white cord, and some collars plain blue.

The Tunic is fastened down the front by eight white metal Buttons carrying the design of three guns horizontal below the Victorian Crown. Cuffs are embellished with an Austrian Knot of red cord and the leading edges and skirts are piped in similar shade material. The blue cloth shoulder straps were piped in red, but carried no distinctive title at that stage. The back of the Jacket had two panels piped with red and embellished with three white metal buttons.

Four of the Volunteers wear a ring of white tape or silver braid on the right arm. This distinction, 0.75″ wide, denotes that the man is an 'Efficient' member of the Corps.

Trousers of similar blue material with a red stripe, 1.75″ wide down each of the outside leg seams, and worn with black boots complete the outfit.

Accoutrements

The Volunteer Gunners wear a white buff leather waistbelt 2″ wide with a white metal rectangular clasp. The Clasp is insufficiently clear to see the exact details, but very likely was of simple design with Grenade ornament. The belt supports a Bayonet Frog and Cap Pouch. Over the left shoulder each Gunner wears a white leather Crossbelt which supports a black leather Ammunition Pouch, the flap of which was usually decorated with a white metal Gun or Grenade ornament.

Notes:

The Bandsman wears the Undress Blue Forage Cap of the Pill Box pattern and a blue tunic frogged with bars of black or scarlet cord.

The Cannon depicted is very likely the Russian piece presented to Caernarfon town as a souvenier of the Crimean War.

FORAGE CAP GRENADE OF THE PATTERN FAVOURED B VOLUNTEER ARTILLERY, 1859-1908. Silver Plated or White Metal finish.

OTHER RANKS BUSBY PLUME HOLDER, VOLUNTEER ARTILLERY 1860-78. WHITE METAL.

OFFICERS BUSBY PLUME HOLDERS. GENERAL PATTERN 1860-78. SILVER or SILVER PLATED FINISH *(N. Litchfield)*

OTHER RANKS HELMET PLATE,
2nd CARNARVONSHIRE ARTILLERY VOLUNTEERS
1878-1880
(Owen Collection)

OTHER RANKS HELMET PLATE,
1st CHESHIRE & CARNARVONSHIRE ARTILLERY VOLUNTEERS,
1880-1904
(Owen Collection)

By kind permission R.W.F. Museum

GENERAL PATTERN ARTILLERY
VOLUNTEER HELMET PLATE WORN
PRE 1902. WHITE METAL OR SILVER
PLATED FINISH
By kind permission of N. Litchfield

ARTILLERY VOLUNTEERS HOME
SERVICE PATTERN BLUE CLOTH
HELMET WITH WHITE METAL FITTINGS
AND WHITE METAL GENERAL PATTERN
PLATE AS WORN PRE 1902
By kind permission of N. Litchfield

Caernarvon Battery RGA Volunteers, c.1908
(By kind permission R.W.F. Museum)

LIEUT. COLONEL HUGH SAVAGE, V.D.
OFFICER COMMANDING BANGOR COMPANY, CHESHIRE AND CARNARVON ARTILLERY VOLUNTEERS. c.1893
(Owen Collection)

THE RIFLE VOLUNTEERS 1860-1863
ANGLESEY

ANGLESEY RIFLE VOLUNTEERS 1860-1863

The Rifle Volunteer movement in Anglesey was somewhat short lived, its demise being the result of several factors, not the least of which was a falling off of interest and opposition from the non conformist element in the County.

In April 1860, an attempt was made to form a Corps in Holyhead, the *Swansea and Glamorgan Herald* on the 25th of the month reporting:

"83 employees of the Steam Packet Depot of the London and North Western Railway Company and the City of Dublin Steam Packet Company have submitted their names." And also "Mr Rigby of the New Harbour Works is to form a Corps from persons in his employ and at his own expense."

In spite of that enthusiasm Mr Rigby and other interested parties did not achieve their military ambitions, probably due to the refusal of the Lord Lieutenant to grant them commissions.

In November of the same year three Corps of Rifle Volunteers had been formed. Locations and Officers were as follows:

1st (Amlwch) Corps

Captain Henry B. Mitchell	6 November, 1860
later, the following were also appointed	
Lieut. John Wynn Paynter	20 December, 1860
Ensign Benjamin Roose	5 April, 1861
Hon. A/Surgeon Thomas D. Griffith, M.D.	5 April, 1861
Hon. Chaplain Rev. Robert Hughes	5 April, 1861

2nd (Aberffraw) Corps

Captain Owen A.F. Meyrick	5 November, 1860

3rd (Menai Bridge) Corps

Captain Robert G. Hughes	2 November, 1860

No details of the numbers enrolled into each Corps have been found, but it is clear that they did not progress sufficiently well to be able to form an Administrative Battalion. No additional Officers were appointed to the Aberffraw and Menai Bridge Corps, and by 1862 both units had been disbanded and were no longer listed in the Monthly Army List. All that remained was the Amlwch Corps, also in a state of decline. In 1863 that unit was also disbanded and was removed from the Army List in December of that year. Anglesey was thereafter not represented by Infantry (Rifle) Volunteers until the turn of the century, when a Company was formed at Holyhead for the 3rd Volunteer Battalion, Royal Welsh Fusiliers.

UNIFORM, BADGES AND INSIGNIA ANGLESEY RIFLE VOLUNTEERS, 1860-63

Little is known about the Uniform, Badges and Insignia of the rather short lived Anglesey Corps other than that they wore a grey Uniform similar in style to that worn by the Scottish Edinburgh Rifle Volunteers.

In The Welsh Folk Museum is a Grey Rifle Volunteer Shako which carries on the inside the inscription 'Anglesey'. On the front is the imprint of a badge, viz, the Plumes, Coronet and Motto of the Prince of Wales. The Badge depicted is of bronze construction and came into the Author's possession some thirty years ago and was marked Anglesey Rifle Volunteers. The Badge and imprint on the Shako described coincide.

(Owen Collection)

CAERNARFONSHIRE RIFLE VOLUNTEERS, 1860-1884

THE INDIVIDUAL CORPS — CARNARVONSHIRE RIFLE VOLUNTEERS

Seven Corps of Rifle Volunteers were raised in the County during March/April, 1860. The precedence of one Corps over another in the County is indicated in the number alloted to it, which was determined by the date on which the Lord Lieutenant received the application to form the Corps and his recommendation to the Secretary of State for War that its services should be accepted.

The date of formation of each of the Corps listed is taken from the Monthly Army Lists, and is the date on which the Officer selected to command the unit was gazetted as Captain Commandant. A comparison with the Muster Rolls which form part of the Porthmadoc MSS (National Library of Wales) shows that the dates of enrolment for the various Corps is more than often later than those extracted from the Army Lists.

1st (Carnarvon) Corps

Major G.S.C.D. Pennant	1 March, 1860
Lieut. John Francis	1 March, 1860

The Muster Roll for this Corps gives April 17th, 1860, as the date when enrolment took place. Its establishment was set at 100 Volunteers — a target which was not achieved. 59 men are listed on April 17th, and a further 28 were added to the Roll between June 1860 and March 22nd, 1861. A Return dated 14th August, 1861, gives the strength as 87 Volunteers, the majority of whom were residents in the parishes of Llanllechid and Llandegai. Two men are listed under Bangor Parish and 6 under Llanddeiniolen. Average age of the Volunteers was 25 — the oldest listed is 37 years of age, and the youngest 19. Most were employees, or connected with the Pennant owned Slate Quarrying interests in the district.

2nd (Carnarvon) Corps

Lieut. Hamilton Alder Roberts	1 March, 1860

The Establishment of this Corps was set at 100 Volunteers, but it does not appear to have exceeded 89 Other Ranks in strength, which total was reached by July 26th, 1861. The men were drawn from the Parishes of Llandegai, Llanllechid and Llanddeiniolen, and like their comrades in the 1st Corps were in the main employees in the Pennant owned Slate Quarries of the district.

3rd (Carnarvon) Corps

Captain Henry Runsey Williams	1 March, 1860
Lieut. John Washington Poole	1 March, 1860
Ensign James Wilmot Rees	1 March, 1860
Hon. A/Surgeon William Maughan	4 December, 1860

Established strength of this Corps was 100 Volunteers, which included 3 Sergeants and 3 Corporals. A Return dated 11th September, 1860, shows the actual strength to be only 54, the men being mainly residents of the Parish of Llanbeblig. For reasons as yet undiscovered, Captain Williams and Lieut. Poole resigned in May 1860 and were succeeded by Captain Richard Fawcett and Lieut. James Wilmot Rees (late Ensign). The vacant Ensigncy was filled by John T. Williams, and all three Commissions are dated 2nd June, 1860. Although enrolled early, it will be noted that the Hon. Surgeon of this and other Corps were not gazetted until 4th December. This was due to uncertainty amongst the Lords Lieutenant of many Counties as to the propriety of granting Volunteer Commissions to members of the Medical profession.

4th (Tremadoc) Corps

Captain Henry Windus Mathews of Penmorfa	1 March, 1860
Lieut. Griffith Humphrey Owen	1 March, 1860
Ensign John Jones of Llanfrothen	1 March, 1860
Hon. A/Surgeon Robert Roberts of Ynyscynhaiarn	4 December, 1860

Established strength set for the Corps was the usual 100 Volunteers, but a Return dated 9th August, 1861, shows that between March 31st, 1860, and January 1861 the Corps for a short period numbered 122 Other Ranks. The novelty of part time soldiering soon wore off, and between August 1860 and July 1861, one Officer and 26 Other Ranks resigned to leave 4 Officers and 82 Other Ranks.

The men were mainly residents of the parish of Ynyscynhaiarn. Only two men are listed under Llanfihangel y Traethau parish on the south side of the Cob. By August 1862, the Corps was by resignations further reduced to 73 Volunteers.

On the resignation of Lieut. G.H. Owen in January 1861, the vacancy was filled by Lieut. John Humphreys Jones.

50 of the 73 Volunteers serving in August 1862 were returned as Effectives.

5th (Pwllheli) Corps

Captain Robert Carreg	1 March, 1860
Lieut. Hugh Hunter Hughes	1 March, 1860
Ensign Hugh Pugh	1 March, 1860
Hon. A/Surgeon Thomas H. Hughes	4 December, 1860

Enrolment commenced 26th March, 1860, and by 16th January, 1861, 64 Volunteers are listed. This figure did not however take into account resignations, the true number serving at that date being more like 58. Ensign Hugh Pugh terminated his service about October 1860, and the vacancy was filled by Ensign Picton Jones on the 26th of that month. By August 1862, 73 men were enrolled in the Corps, 70 of which were returned as Effective.

The Armoury in Pwllheli contained at that date 66 Long Enfield Rifles and Bayonets, 4 Short Enfield Rifles and Bayonets and a quantity of Armourer's Tools and Stores.

The Volunteers forming this Corps were in 1860 drawn almost entirely from the parish of Denio, with one man only listed under Abererch. Bottwnog parish later provided one or two men for the Corps.

6th (Bangor) Corps

Captain Pennant Athel Iremonger	3 March, 1860
Lieut. John William Hughes	3 March, 1860
Ensign William Pritchard	3 March,1860
Hon. A/Surgeon Thomas H. Hughes	4 December, 1860

The founder of this Corps and its Captain Commandant was also Adjutant of the County Regiment of Militia. Enrolment commenced March 7th, 1860, and a Return dated August 1860 shows its enrolled strength to be 60 Volunteers, 55 of whom were returned as Efficient. The men were drawn mainly from Bangor parish with one or two listed under Llandegai. A slight increase in numbers is recorded by October 1861 when 63 Volunteers represent the enrolled strength, 54 of which were returned as Efficient.

7th (Conway) Corps

Captain James Edwards of Conway	4 April, 1860
Lieut. Robert Farrant of Llandudno	4 April, 1860
Ensign Vernon Darbishire of Dwygyfylchi	4 April, 1860
Hon. A/Surgeon John Salisbury of Conway	4 December, 1860

Enrolment for this Corps (Established strength 100) commenced 26th April, 1860. A Return dated August 1860 shows enrolled strength to be 4 Officers and 87 Other Ranks, drawn from residents of the Parishes of Conway, Llandudno and Caerhun. The following men are listed as Sergeants:

S.O. Williams, Llandudno
Thomas Morrell, Llandudno
Edward Jones, Dwygyfylchi
Edward Polin, Dwygyfylchi

By August 1861, the Corps was reduced by resignations to 64 Volunteers.

Note:
A person making reference to the Monthly Army Lists for 1860-62 could be misled into thinking that the 1st, 2nd and 3rd Corps were all Carnarvon based, whereas in fact only the 3rd Corps was based upon the County Town where the Parish of Llanbeblig (beblick) extended to include Waenfawr and Bontnewydd. Only in 1862 are the 1st and 2nd Corps' locations more accurately described as Penrhyn. The 4th (Tremadoc) Corps in taking in Llanfrothen and Llanfihangel y Traethau also touched upon Merionethshire. The 7th (Conway) Corps also extended from Penmaenmawr (Dwygyfylchi), to Conway and the district south of the town and across to include Llandudno.

MUSTER ROLL — 1st (CARNARVON) CORPS — 14th AUGUST, 1861

NAME	PARISH	DATE ENROLLED
Thomas Birch	Llandegai	17.4.1860
Robert Lewis	Llanllechid	17.4.1860
Hugh Jones	Llandegai	17.4.1860
Richard Hughes	Llanllechid	17.4.1860
Hugh Parry	Llanllechid	17.4.1860
Thomas Jones	Llandegai	17.4.1860
John Jones	Llanllechid	17.4.1860
John Thomas	Llandegai	17.4.1860
Hugh Jones	Llanllechid	17.4.1860
David Jones	Llanddeiniolen	17.4.1860
Thomas Hughes	Llanllechid	17.4.1860
Thomas M. Hughes	Llanllechid	17.4.1860
Thomas Davies	Llandegai	17.4.1860
David Jones	Llandegai	17.4.1860
Elias Williams	Llanllechid	17.4.1860
Morgan Thomas	Llanllechid	17.4.1860
Morris Owen Price	Llanllechid	17.4.1860
Moses Jones	Llandegai	17.4.1860
Robert Jones	Llanllechid	17.4.1860
William Ellis	Llandegai	17.4.1860
Owen Hughes	Llandegai	17.4.1860
Thomas Jones	Llanllechid	17.4.1860
Owen Owens	Llanllechid	17.4.1860
William Williams	Llanllechid	17.4.1860
Edward J. Edwards	Llanllechid	17.4.1860
Evan Thomas	Llandegai	17.4.1860
John Williams	Llandegai	17.4.1860
William Jones	Llandegai	17.4.1860
John Griffith	Llanddeiniolen	17.4.1860
William Williams	Bangor	17.4.1860
Richard J. Price	Llanllechid	17.4.1860
John Roberts	Llandegai	17.4.1860
Henry Williams	Llanllechid	17.4.1860
Thomas Evans	Llanllechid	17.4.1860

Elias Jones	Llanllechid	17.4.1860
Daniel Griffith	Llanllechid	17.4.1860
William Jones	Llanllechid	17.4.1860
Robert Thomas	Llanllechid	17.4.1860
Hugh Jones	Llanllechid	17.4.1860
Robert Thomas	Llandegai	17.4.1860
Thomas Owens	Llandegai	17.4.1860
Edwin Davies	Llandegai	17.4.1860
Griffith Thomas	Llanllechid	17.4.1860
Thomas Roberts	Llandegai	17.4.1860
William Hughes	Llanllechid	17.4.1860
Robert Williams	Llandegai	17.4.1860
John Tuigge	Llandegai	17.4.1860
Robert Williams	Llanddeiniolen	17.4.1860
Robert Hughes	Llandegai	17.4.1860
Robert Roberts	Bangor	17.4.1860
Evan Jones	Llanddeiniolen	17.4.1860
Edward Owens	Llanddeiniolen	17.4.1860
Thomas J. Roberts	Llanllechid	17.4.1860
Morris Williams	Llanddeiniolen	17.4.1860
Robert Evans	Llanllechid	17.4.1860
Hugh Roberts	Llandegai	17.4.1860
Robert Rowlands	Llandegai	17.4.1860
John Williams	Llanllechid	17.4.1860
Benjamin Pritchard	Llandegai	16.6.1860
William Owens	Llanllechid	16.6.1860
Jacob Parry	Llanllechid	16.6.1860
William Griffith	Llanllechid	16.6.1860
Thomas Williams	Llanllechid	29.10.1860
David Parry	Llanllechid	17.4.1860
Griffith Jones	Llandegai	17.4.1860
William Jones	Llandegai	17.4.1860
Griffith Morris	Llandegai	17.4.1860
Daniel Thomas	Llandegai	17.4.1860
John Pritchard	Llandegai	16.6.1860
John Pritchard	Llanllechid	16.6.1860
Owen Jones	Llanllechid	16.6.1860
John Owens	Llandegai	16.6. 1860
Robert Morris	Llanllechid	16.6.1860
Thomas Williams	Llandegai	20.10.1860
Hugh Williams	Llandegai	16.6.1860
Roberts Parry	Llandegai	29.10.1860
William Williams	Llandegai	29.10.1860
David Jones	Llanllechid	29.10.1860

Owen Price	Llanllechid	29.10.1860
Thomas Williams	Llandegai	29.1.1861
John Parry	Llanllechid	29.1.1861
John Gough	Llanllechid	29.1.1861
Edward Parry	Llanddeiniolen	29.1.1861
Griffith Jones	Llanllechid	22.3.1861
John Griffith	Llanllechid	22.3.1861

(Porthmadoc MSS — National Library of Wales)

MUSTER ROLL — 2nd (CARNARVON) CORPS — 31st AUGUST, 1860

NAME	PARISH	DATE ENROLLED
William Thomas	Llandegai	17.4.1860
John Hughes	Llanddeiniolen	17.4.1860
Thomas Roberts	Llanllechid	17.4.1860
John Jones	Llandegai	17.4.1860
William Griffith	Llanllechid	17.4.1860
Hugh Davies	Llandegai	17.4.1860
William Williams	Llanllechid	17.4.1860
John Pritchard	Llandegai	17.4.1860
William Morris	Llanllechid	17.4.1860
William Williams	Llanllechid	17.4.1860
David Joseph	Llanllechid	17.4.1860
Robert Williams	Llanllechid	17.4.1860
Evan Jones	Llanllechid	17.4.1860
Edward Meshach	Llanllechid	17.4.1860
John Jones	Llanllechid	17.4.1860
William Roberts	Llandegai	17.4.1860
Griffith Williams	Llanllechid	17.4.1860
Richard Williams	Llanllechid	17.4.1860
Griffith Roberts	Llanllechid	17.4.1860
John Hughes	Llandegai	17.4.1860
William Williams	Llanddeiniolen	17.4.1860
Humphrey Hughes	Llandegai	17.4.1860
Thomas Williams	Llanddeiniolen	17.4.1860
Lewis Jones	Llandegai	17.4.1860
Nathaniel Williams	Llanddeiniolen	17.4.1860
Henry Owen	Llanllechid	17.17.4.1860
John Pritchard	Llanllechid	17.4.1860
John Williams	Llanddeiniolen	17.4.1860
William Jones	Llandegai	17.4.1860
Thomas Morris	Llanllechid	17.4.1860
William Williams	Llanllechid	17.4.1860
John Humphreys	Llandegai	17.4.1860
John Hughes	Llandegai	17.4.1860
Owen Pritchard	Llanllechid	17.4.1860

William Howell	Llanllechid	17.4.1860
William Hughes	Llandegai	17.4.1860
Owen Owens	Bangor	17.4.1860
Robert Davies	Llandegai	17.4.1860
William Thomas	Llanllechid	17.4.1860
Richard Jones	Llanllechid	17.4.1860
Thomas Knowles	Llanllechid	17.4.1860
William Owen	Llandegai	17.4.1860
Edward Edwards	Llandegai	17.4.1860
William Williams	Llandegai	17.4.1860
John Jones	Llandegai	17.4.1860
Thomas Hughes	Llanllechid	17.4.1860
William Williams	Llandegai	17.4.1860
Lewis Jones	Llanllechid	17.4.1860
William Price	Llanllechid	17.4.1860
William Parry	Llandegai	17.4.1860
Thomas Lewis	Llandegai	17.4.1860
William Roberts	Llanllechid	17.4.1860
Robert Jones	Llandegai	17.4.1860
John Roberts	Llandegai	17.4.1860
Thomas Pritchard	Llandegai	17.4.1860
Griffith Jones	Llanllechid	17.4.1860
Owen Thomas	Llanllechid	17.4.1860
William John Thomas	Llanllechid	17.4.1860
John Roberts	Llanllechid	17.4.1860
William Williams	Llanllechid	17.4.1860
William Roberts	Llanllechid	17.4.1860
Hugh Griffith	Llanllechid	17.4.1860
Robert Thomas	Llanllechid	17.4.1860
Hugh Hughes	Llandegai	17.4.1860
Griffith Williams	Llanllechid	17.4.1860
William Jones	Llanllechid	17.4.1860
Hugh Jones	Llanllechid	17.4.1860
Hugh Hughes	Llanllechid	17.4.1860
William Rowlands	Llanllechid	16.6.1860
Robert Owen	Llanllechid	16.6.1860
Robert Edwards	Llanllechid	16.6.1860
John Morris	Llanllechid	16.6.1860
Henry Williams	Llanllechid	16.6.1860
Owen Williams	Llandegai	16.6.1860
Griffith Jones	Llandegai	16.6.1860
Owen Roberts	Llandegai	16.6.1860
Elias Pritchard	Llandegai	16.6.1860
William Roberts	Llanllechid	16.6.1860

William William Jones	Llanllechid	16.6.1860
William Jones	Llanllechid	16.6.1860
Thomas Thomas	Llandegai	16.6.1860
John Thomas	Llandegai	16.6.1860
William Edwards	Llanllechid	26.7.1860
John Robert Hughes	Llandegai	26.7.1860
Hugh Hughes	Llandegai	26.7.1860
Elias Jones	Llanllechid	26.7.1860
William Williams	Llandegai	26.7.1860
William Pritchard	Llandegai	26.7.1860

(Porthmadoc MSS — National Library of Wales)

MUSTER ROLL — 3rd (CARNARVON) CORPS — 11th SEPTEMBER, 1860

NAME	PARISH	DATE ENROLLED
T. Llewelyn Rees	Llanbeblig	29.3.1860
H.H. Williams	Llanbeblig	29.3.1860
A.D. Jones	Llanbeblig	29.3.1860
Richard Jones	Llanbeblig	29.3.1860
R.D. Williams	Llanbeblig	29.3.1860
John Jones	Llanbeblig	29.3.1860
Pierce Hope	Llanbeblig	29.3.1860
William Roberts	Llanbeblig	29.3.1860
William Hamer	Llanbeblig	29.3.1860
Evan Stephens	Llanbeblig	29.3.1860
William Paynter	Llanbeblig	29.3.1860
J.G. Jones	Llanbeblig	29.3.1860
Thomas Windsor	Llanbeblig	29.3.1860
George Owen	Llanbeblig	29.3.1860
William Clewlow	Llanbeblig	29.3.1860
John Williams	Llanbeblig	29.3.1860
William Owen	Llanbeblig	29.3.1860
Owen Ellis	Llanbeblig	29.3.1860
William Roberts	Llanbeblig	29.3.1860
Griffith Davies	Llanbeblig	29.3.1860
John Pierce	Llanbeblig	23.7.1860
Owen Roberts	Llanbeblig	23.7.1860
Thomas Sneed	Llanbeblig	29.3.1860
Hugh Jones	Llanbeblig	29.3.1860
H.M. Lloyd	Llanbeblig	29.3.1860
C. Evans	Llanbeblig	29.3.1860
John Williams	Clynnog	29.3.1860
John Parry	Llanbeblig	29.3.1860
James Jones	Llanbeblig	29.3.1860
R.N. Jones	Llanbeblig	29.3.1860
W.H. Pritchard	Llanbeblig	29.3.1860
George Pritchard	Llanbeblig	29.3.1860
Owen Morgan	Llanbeblig	29.3.1860
Thomas Morgan	Llanbeblig	29.3.1860

John Lloyd	Llanbeblig	16.4.1860
James Thompson	Llanbeblig	16.4.1860
D. Marshall	Llanbeblig	16.4.1860
John Hughes	Llanbeblig	16.4.1860
W.J. Griffiths	Llanbeblig	16.4.1860
Thomas Lawrey	Llanbeblig	16.4.1860
John Morgan	Llanbeblig	16.4.1860
Griffith Griffith	Llanbeblig	19.4.1860
D. Hamer	Llanbeblig	19.4.1860
R.W. Griffith	Llanbeblig	19.4.1860
D. Morgan	Llanbeblig	19.4.1860
W.T. Jones	Llanbeblig	19.4.1860
E. Evans	Llanbeblig	19.4.1860
D. Parry	Llanbeblig	19.4.1860
Owen Thomas	Llanbeblig	19.4.1860
Robert Lewis	Llanbeblig	24.4.1860
David Evans	Llanbeblig	24.4.1860
Robert Roberts	Llanbeblig	24.4.1860
John Roberts	Llanbeblig	24.4.1860
A.H. de Burgh	Llanbeblig	24.4.1860

A James Reen and J.H. Greathead are also mentioned but not numbered as members of the Corps. They may both have been Honorary Members i.e., persons giving financial support to the unit, allowed to wear the Uniform Dress, but taking no active part in its activities.

MUSTER ROLL — 4th (TREMADOC) CORPS — 9th APRIL, 1861

NAME	PARISH	DATE ENROLLED
Edward Windus Mathew	Penmorfa	31.3.1860
John Humphreys Jones	Ynyscynhaiarn	31.3.1860
John Jones	Llanfrothen	31.3.1860
Robert Roberts	Ynyscynhaiarn	31.3.1860
Henry Humphreys	Ynyscynhaiarn	31.3.1860
John Servis	Ynyscynhaiarn	31.3.1860
William Owen	Ynyscynhaiarn	31.3.1860
John Jones	Ynyscynhaiarn	31.3.1860
Hugh Davies	Ynyscynhaiarn	31.3.1860
Ellis Williams	Ynyscynhaiarn	31.3.1860
Edward Evans	Ynyscynhaiarn	31.3.1860
Edward Owen	Ynyscynhaiarn	31.3.1860
Thomas Jones	Ynyscynhaiarn	31.3.1860
Henry Williams	Ynyscynhaiarn	31.3.1860
Richard Williams	Ynyscynhaiarn	31.3.1860
Evan Jones	Ynyscynhaiarn	31.3.1860
William Williams Lloyd	Ynyscynhaiarn	31.3.1860
William Williams	Llanfihangel-y-Traethau	31.3.1860
William Owen	Ynyscynhaiarn	31.3.1860
Thomas Jones Williams (Sgt)	Ynyscynhaiarn	31.3.1860
Owen Morris Roberts	Ynyscynhaiarn	31.3.1860
William Williams	Ynyscynhaiarn	31.3.1860
John Jones	Ynyscynhaiarn	31.3.1860
Lewis Owen	Ynyscynhaiarn	31.3.1860
David Homfray (Sgt)	Ynyscynhaiarn	5.4.1860
David Evans	Ynyscynhaiarn	7.4.1860
Lewis Hughes	Ynyscynhaiarn	13.4.1860
Robert Lloyd	Ynyscynhaiarn	13.4.1860
Morris Isaac	Ynyscynhaiarn	13.4.1860
Griffith Morris	Ynyscynhaiarn	19.5.1860
Evan Evans	Ynyscynhaiarn	17.7.1860
Frederick Ash (Sgt)	Ynyscynhaiarn	17.7.1860
John Davies	Ynyscynhaiarn	21.7.1860

Richard Jones	Ynyscynhaiarn	21.7.1860
Evan Williams	Ynyscynhaiarn	3.9.1860
Richard Williams	Ynyscynhaiarn	3.9.1860
Daniel Morris	Ynyscynhaiarn	3.9.1860
William Roberts	Ynyscynhaiarn	12.10.1860
Job Thomas	Ynyscynhaiarn	12.10.1860
Hugh Williams	Ynyscynhaiarn	27.11.1860
William Williams	Ynyscynhaiarn	17.1.1861
Griffith Griffith Page	Ynyscynhaiarn	19.1.1861
Job Thomas	Ynyscynhaiarn	19.1.1861
Thomas Ffoulkes	Ynyscynhaiarn	13.5.1861
Griffith H. Jones	Ynyscynhaiarn	22.5.1861
John Owen	Ynyscynhaiarn	4.6.1861
John Williams Roberts	Ynyscynhaiarn	15.6.1861
Robert Pritchard	Ynyscynhaiarn	25.6.1861
Benjamin Wyatt (Sgt)	Ynyscynhaiarn	24.8.1861
Thomas Casson (Sgt)	Ynyscynhaiarn	1.10.1861

(Porthmadoc MSS — National Library of Wales)

MUSTER ROLL — 5th (PWLLHELI) CORPS — 12th SEPTEMBER, 1860

NAME	PARISH	DATE ENROLLED
George Maclean	Abererch	26.3.1860
Richard Evans	Abererch	3.4.1860
Griffith Thomas Picton Jones	Abererch	9.4.1860
Albert Jenkin	Bottwnog	9.4.1860
Thomas Hunter Hughes	Denio	26.3.1860
William G. Casson	Denio	26.3.1860
William Price	Denio	26.3.1860
Evan Evans	Denio	26.3.1860
James Williams	Denio	26.3.1860
Griffith Hughes	Denio	26.3.1860
John Toleman	Denio	26.3.1860
John Edwards	Denio	26.3.1860
William Cadwalader Williams	Denio	29.3.1860
Dafydd Wynn Williams	Denio	28.3.1860
Lewis Williams	Denio	18.5.1860
Rice Owen Pugh	Denio	26.3.1860
Owen Owen	Denio	26.3.1860
David Pugh Edwards	Denio	26.3.1860
John Williams	Denio	26.3.1860
Thomas Luckman	Denio	26.3.1860
William Blackburn	Denio	26.3.1860
Evan Tomas Evans	Denio	4.4.1860
Thomas Lloyd	Denio	20.4.1860
Henry Hughes	Denio	30.3.1860
John Owens	Denio	27.3.1860
William Evans	Denio	26.3.1860
Owen Roberts	Denio	30.3.1860
Richard Griffith	Denio	2.4.1860
John Evans	Denio	28.3.1860
Humphrey Griffith	Denio	29.3.1860
Robert Evans	Denio	28.3.1860
Griffith Griffiths	Denio	27.3.1860

John Jones	Denio	3.4.1860
Robert Roberts	Denio	26.3.1860
William Meredith Williams	Denio	16.4.1860
John Owen	Denio	27.3.1860
Robert Hughes	Denio	26.3.1860
Owen Hughes	Denio	11.4.1860
David Evans	Denio	28.3.1860
Griffith Williams	Denio	11.4.1860
Humphrey Jones	Denio	20.4.1860
Hugh Roberts	Denio	21.5.1860
Owen Williams	Denio	29.3.1860
Thomas Davies	Denio	30.4.1860
David Jones	Denio	4.4.1860
Robert Jones	Denio	4.6.1860
Thomas Jones	Denio	28.3.1860
Morris Roberts	Denio	26.3.1860
Edward Roberts	Denio	7.7.1860
Robert Morgan	Denio	11.4.1860
William Williams	Denio	21.7.1860
Daniel Pierce	Denio	21.7.1860
Robert Pierce	Denio	21.7.1860
Zechariah Humphries	Denio	21.7.1860
William Williams	Denio	21.7.1860
Richard Griffith	Denio	18.4.1860
William Phillip Jones	Denio	18.4.1860
John Roberts	Denio	18.4.1860

(Porthmadoc MSS — National Library of Wales)

MUSTER ROLL — 6th (BANGOR) CORPS — AUGUST 1860

NAME	PARISH	DATE ENROLLED
John Williams	Bangor	7.3.1860
Frederick Mathews	Bangor	7.3.1860
Robert Hughes	Bangor	7.3.1860
Richard Llewelyn Griffiths	Bangor	7.3.1860
Evan Evans	Bangor	7.3.1860
Robert Roberts	Bangor	7.3.1860
John Pritchard	Bangor	7.3.1860
Watson Robinson	Bangor	7.3.1860
William R. Thomas	Bangor	7.3.1860
William Roberts	Bangor	7.3.1860
Robert Stewart	Bangor	7.3.1860
William Pritchard	Bangor	7.3.1860
John L. Jones	Bangor	7.3.1860
W.P. Lewis	Bangor	7.3.1860
Thomas G. Hardie	Bangor	7.3.1860
William Pritchard	Bangor	7.3.1860
John Timothy	Llandenlio	7.3.1860
Henry Harrison	Bangor	7.3.1860
Richard Henry Roberts	Bangor	7.3.1860
Zachariah Roberts	Bangor	7.3.1860
Samuel Hughes	Bangor	7.3.1860
John Pilgrim Morris	Bangor	7.3.1860
Robert Mopson	Bangor	7.3.1860
Owen Thomas Williams	Bangor	7.3.1860
John Williams	Bangor	7.3.1860
John Evan Roberts	Bangor	7.3.1860
Edward Pugh	Bangor	7.3.1860
David Lewis Dale	Bangor	7.3.1860
John Williams	Bangor	7.3.1860
Thomas Thomas	Bangor	7.3.1860
Evan Evans	Bangor	7.3.1860
Griffith Davies	Bangor	7.3.1860
William Thomas	Llandegai	7.3.1860

Thomas Thomas Parry	Bangor	7.3.1860
Mesach Roberts	Bangor	7.3.1860
Joseph Williams	Bangor	7.3.1860
Pennant A. Iremonger	Llandegai	7.3.1860
Arthur W. Hodom	Bangor	9.3.1860
John Ambrose Jones	Bangor	14.3.1860
Edmund Buckland	Bangor	14.3.1860
John Brown	Bangor	14.3.1860
Robert Thomas	Llandegai	14.3.1860
John Thomas	Bangor	24.4.1860
Isaac Roberts	Bangor	24.4.1860
William Owens	Bangor	24.4.1860
David Hughes	Bangor	24.3.1860
John William Hughes	Bangor	24.3.1860
Thomas Williams	Bangor	24.3.1860
John Bolus	Bangor	27.4.1860
William Roberts	Bangor	5.6.1860
Lewis A. Curnon	Bangor	23.7.1860
John William Jones	Bangor	23.7.1860
Frederick A.	Bangor	7.3.1860
William George Young	Bangor	7.3.1860
Mathew Hughes	Bangor	7.3.1860
Thomas Evans	Bangor	7.3.1860
Robert Griffiths	Bangor	7.3.1860
John Lloyd	Bangor	7.3.1860
William Jones	Bangor	7.3.1860
John Jones	Bangor	7.3.1860

MUSTER ROLL — 7th (CONWAY) CORPS, CARNARVONSHIRE RIFLE VOLUNTEERS, 1860

NUMBER	PARISH	NAME	DATE ENROLLED
	Benarth, Conway	James Edwards. Capt.	26.4.1860
	Llandudno	Robert Farrant. Lieut.	26.4.1860
	Dwygyfylchi	Vernon Darbishire. Ens.	26.4.1860
	Conway	John Salisbury. Asst. Surg.	26.4.1860
1.	Gyffin	Thomas H. Wheeler	26.4.1860
2.	Conway	William Hughes	26.4.1860
3.	Caerhun	H.E. Sullivan	26.4.1860
4.	Conway	William Owen	26.4.1860
5.	Conway	Hugh David	26.4.1860
6.	Conway	William Jones	26.4.1860
7.	Conway	Robert Foulkes	26.4.1860
8.	Conway	W.P. Williams	26.4.1860
9.	Dwygyfylchi	Edmond Jones	26.4.1860
10.	Dwygyfylchi	Robert Maitland	26.4.1860
11.	Dwygyfylchi	Isaac Blinkinsop	26.4.1860
12.	Dwygyfylchi	Thomas Lawson	26.4.1860
13.	Dwygyfylchi	Hugh Jones	26.4.1860
14.	Conway	Moses Williams	26.4.1860
15.	Conway	Moses Roberts	26.4.1860
16.	Conway	William H. Wilson	26.4.1860
17.	Conway	Walter Neve	26.4.1860
18.	Conway	Thomas Jones	26.4.1860
19.	Conway	Owen Jones	26.4.1860
20.	Dwygyfylchi	Edward Polin	26.4.1860
21.	Llandudno	S.O. Williams	26.4.1860
22.	Llandudno	Daniel Phillips	26.4.1860
23.	Llandudno	William Hayden	26.4.1860
24.	Llandudno	Thomas Movile	26.4.1860
25.	Llandudno	David Lloyd	26.4.1860
26.	Llandudno	Samuel Lily	26.4.1860
27.	Llandudno	Thomas Broakes	26.4.1860
28.	Llandudno	William Pritchard	26.4.1860
29.	Llandudno	Thomas Evans	26.4.1860

30.	Llandudno	William Lester	26.4.1860
31.	Llandudno	George Edwin Jones	26.4.1860
32.	Llandudno	Henry Parr	26.4.1860
33.	Llandudno	J.W. Edgecombe	26.4.1860
34.	Llandudno	Hugh Hughes	26.4.1860
35.	Llandudno	William Allen	26.4.1860
36.	Llandudno	William Evans	26.4.1860
37.	Llandudno	Joseph Pritchard	26.4.1860
38.	Llandudno	David Jones	26.4.1860
39.	Llandudno	John Johnson	26.4.1860
40.	Llandudno	Charles Lloyd	26.4.1860
41.	Llandudno	Richard Conway	26.4.1860
42.	Llandudno	Thomas Johnson	26.4.1860
43.	Llandudno	Robert Williams	26.4.1860
44.	Llandudno	Thomas Williams	26.4.1860
45.	Llandudno	Charles Collins	26.4.1860
46.	Llandudno	John Broothes	26.4.1860
47.	Llandudno	Edward Thomas	26.4.1860
48.	Llandudno	Isiah Davies	26.4.1860
49.	Llandudno	Geoffrey Jones	26.4.1860
50.	Llandudno	William Roberts	26.4.1860
51.	Llandudno	John Sharpe	26.4.1860
52.	Llandudno	John Davies	26.4.1860
53.	Llandudno	Samuel Broothes	26.4.1860
54.	Llandudno	Thomas Newton	26.4.1860
55.	Llandudno	Henry Staveley	26.4.1860
56.	Llandudno	William Powell	26.4.1860
57.	Llandudno	Thomas Jones	26.4.1860
58.	Llandudno	Joseph Jones	26.4.1860
59.	Llandudno	William Williams	26.4.1860
60.	Llandudno	Hugh Jones	26.4.1860
61.	Llandudno	W.A. Darbishire	4.8.1860
62.	Llandudno	Charles Stuckley	4.8.1860
63.	Caerhun	I. Ramsden	11.8.1860
64.	Caerhun	John Davies	11.8.1860
65.	Caerhun	Edward Evans	11.8.1860
66.	Caerhun	Griffith Davies	11.8.1860
67.	Caerhun	Rowland Roberts	11.8.1860
68.	Caerhun	William Roberts	11.8.1860
69.	Caerhun	John Williams	11.8.1860
70.	Caerhun	William Jones	11.8.1860
71.	Caerhun	William Roberts	11.8.1860
72.	Caerhun	Griffith Williams	11.8.1860
73.	Caerhun	John Jones	11.8.1860

74.	Caerhun	David Thomas	11.8.1860
75.	Caerhun	Ernest Evans	11.8.1860
76.	Caerhun	William Mesach	11.8.1860
77.	Caerhun	Robert Owen	11.8.1860
78.	Caerhun	Henry Williams	11.8.1860
79.	Caerhun	Robert Davies	11.8.1860
80.	Caerhun	William Owen Pritchard	11.8.1860
81.	Caerhun	John Morris Jones	11.8.1860
82.	Caerhun	Mathew Roberts	11.8.1860
83.	Caerhun	John Parry	11.8.1860
84.	Caerhun	John Parry Jones	11.8.1860
85.	Caerhun	William Owen	11.8.1860
86.	Caerhun	Henry Kersey	11.8.1860
87.	Caerhun	John Roberts	11.8.1860

1st ADMINISTRATIVE BATTALION, CARNARVONSHIRE RIFLE VOLUNTEERS, 1860-1873

On August 2nd, 1860, the seven Carnarvonshire Corps of Rifle Volunteers were grouped together to form an Administrative Battalion, the object of which according to a Memorandum dated 4th September, 1860, was to "unite the different Corps composing it under one common head, to secure uniformity of drill amongst them, and to afford them the advantage of the instruction and assistance of an Adjutant."

In no way did the change interfere with the financial arrangements or rules of the respective Corps, neither did it compel them to meet together for Battalion Drill in ordinary times, unless by common consent.

The Headquarters of the Battalion was located in Caernarfon, with G.S.G.D. Pennant as Major Commandant and with Captain Wildman Yates Peel as Adjutant.

In 1862, the 1st and 2nd Corps hitherto sub-titled Carnarvon became the 1st (Penrhyn) and 2nd (Penrhyn) Corps, but the Army List of March 1863 shows that both were somewhat short on Officers. Command of the 1st was vested in Lieut. John Francis and that of the 2nd, in Lieut. H.A. Roberts — no other Officers appearing under either body.

In the 4th Corps at Tremadoc, Lieut. G.H. Owen had been succeeded by Lieut. John Humphrey Jones as from 8th June, 1861, whilst in Pwllheli the 5th Corps was commanded by Captain Hugh Hunter Hughes, promoted Captain Commandant, 6th August, 1861, and assisted by:

Lieut. Griffith T. Picton Jones	13 September, 1861
and Ensign William Gasson	13 September, 1861

whilst Thomas H. Hughes remained in post as Hon. Assistant Surgeon. In the 6th Corps at Bangor, Captain Iremonger had been succeeded by Captain John William Hughes with effect 12th September, 1861. His Lieutenant as from 13th September of the same year was William Pritchard one time Ensign in the Corps. John Salisbury remained in post as Hon. Assistant Surgeon.

In the 7th Corps only Lieut. Henry Eden Sullivan (14th June, 1861) is listed with Lieut. Vernon Darbishire (14th June, 1861) as Supernumerary. As in Anglesey, the Non-Conformist influence and a decline in interest led to a falling off in numbers. This resulted in the disbandment of the 6th (Bangor) Corps which no longer appears in the Army List after September 1865. By December 1866, the Conway Corps had also been obliged to call it a day.

On October 3rd, 1868, Edward Windus Mathew succeeded Major Pennant as Officer Commanding the Administrative Battalion whilst still retaining command of the 4th (Tremadoc) Corps. The Army List of November 1869 gives the following Battalion state:

1st (Penrhyn) Corps

Captain John Francis	20 December, 1866

2nd (Penrhyn) Corps

Captain Hamilton Alder Roberts	20 December, 1866

3rd (Carnarvon) Corps

Captain John T. Williams	9 November, 1867
Lieut. Owen Thomas	19 December, 1868
Hon. A/Surgeon William Maughan	4 December, 1860

4th (Tremadoc) Corps

Captain Edward Windus Mathew	1 March,1860
also Major Commandant of the Administrative Battalion.	
Lieut. John Humphrey Jones	8 June, 1861
Ensign David Homfray	4 December, 1860
Hon. A/Surgeon Robert Roberts	4 December, 1860

5th (Pwllheli) Corps

Captain Griffith T. Picton Jones	18 October, 1864
Lieut. Thomas Hunter Hughes	24 October, 1865
Hon. A/Surgeon Thomas H. Hughes	4 December, 1860

Since the date of their formation, the activities of the various Rifle Volunteer Corps concentrated mainly on proficiency in musketry, which practice took place on ranges set up at various suitable local sites. Occasionally the various Corps came together for Battalion Drill, Reviews, Inspections, but as individual units they featured greatly at local functions particularly during the 'Volunteer Season' which extended roughly from Easter to October in each year.

With the exception of heavily populated and industrial districts the men involved were mainly from a middle class or artisan background: this mainly due to the costs involved, as in addition to being expected to pay entrance fees and annual subscriptions, Volunteers were expected to provide their own Uniform Dress, and in the formative days, in many instances, their own Rifles. To be classed as an 'Efficient' was of utmost importance, as by that attainment a Volunteer earned for his Corps a Government Capitation Grant which offset the overall expense of running the unit.

To begin with, the Volunteer Force was not seen as a body expected to take to the Field en masse to confront an invader, but more as a supporting arm to the regular army, with ability to skirmish, scout and by making use of local knowledge, harass the enemy lines of communication. General regulations and Instructions dated July 2nd, 1873, divided the United Kingdom into 70 Infantry Sub-Districts, and to each Sub-District Brigade were alloted for recruiting purpose two Line Battalions (Regulars) as also the Militia and Volunteers of the area. This was a step towards bringing about a much closer linking of the Volunteers with the Regular Army.

THE CARNARVONSHIRE ELEMENT, 1st ADMINISTRATIVE BATTALION, FLINTSHIRE RIFLE VOLUNTEERS, 1873-1880

The declining strength of the Carnarvonshire Administrative Battalion led in 1873 to its being broken up, and it last appears in the Army List in December of that year. From January 1874, the five remaining Corps of Carnarvonshire Rifle Volunteers are shown as being united to the 1st Administrative Battalion, Flintshire Rifle Volunteers. The reorganisation did not affect the autonomy of the Caernarfonshire Corps, but ensured some cost cutting, and for them the services of the Adjutant of the Flintshire Battalion.

The year 1875 saw the disbandment of the 1st (Penrhyn) Corps, and 1877 the disappearance of the 2nd (Penrhyn) and 5th (Pwllheli). In 1878 however, a new Corps was raised in Llanberis and numbered 5th, and so ensured that the County contribution was maintained at an acceptable level.

1st FLINTSHIRE AND CARNARVONSHIRE RIFLE VOLUNTEER CORPS, 1880-1884

In February 1880, the various Corps administered by the Flintshire Administrative Battalion were consolidated to form Companies of the 1st Flintshire Rifle Volunteer Corps, which Battalion was in March of the same year redesignated 1st Flintshire and Carnarvonshire Rifle Volunteer Corps. In this new organisation the Caernarfonshire contribution consisted of:

'G' and 'H' Companies — late 3rd (Carnarvon) Corps
'I' Company — late 4th (Tremadoc) Corps
'K' Company — late 5th (Llanberis) Corps

Headquarters of 'I' Company had by this date been relocated in Portmadoc, but the old title is included here to avoid confusion.

COLOURS

Article 135 of the Volunteer Regulations of 1863 state: "Neither Standards nor Colours are to be carried by Corps on parade, as the Volunteer Force is composed of arms to which their use is not appropriate." This is not to say that Colours were not acquired by certain Corps of Rifle Volunteers, as there are surviving examples which were presented in the 1860s to at least two Welsh Corps. They were however quite unofficial, being the handiwork of wellwishers and ladies associated with the membership.

No record of any such presentation to a Carnarvonshire Corps or its successor has been found, and no example has to date been sighted.

UNIFORM, BADGES AND INSIGNIA CARNARVONSHIRE RIFLE VOLUNTEERS AND SUCCESSORS 1860-1884

The North Wales Chronicle, 11th February, 1860, tells us that the Carnarvonshire Rifle Volunteer Corps wore a Grey uniform — a shade much favoured by the Rifle Volunteers of the day. That grey was worn by the 1st Corps is confirmed by a painting of Major G.S. Douglas Pennant of Penrhyn Castle now preserved in the Regimental Museum of the Royal Welsh Fusiliers and which can be described as follows:

HEAD-DRESS

A grey cloth Shako of style similar to that worn by Line Infantry of the day with black patent leather peak and black patent chin strap and the crown at front is adorned with a plume of black cock feathers. On the front is displayed the Corps Shako Plate — circular in shape and topped with the Victorian Crown. On the plate in relief, the Welsh Dragon, guardaunt, within a closed wreath of laurel. The whole bronzed.

UNIFORM

A grey tunic with scarlet collar and cuffs fastened with eight bronze buttons at the front. The shoulders carry black intertwined shoulder cords and the collar is edged in similar material. The pointed cuffs are edged in black cord which culminates both above and below in decorative knots: the cord at cuff edge and knot above edged with ornamental tracing. The single breasted jacket is worn with grey trousers of similar shade decorated on the outside leg seam with a broad black stripe.

ACCOUTREMENTS

Major Pennant wears a black patent leather belt with bronze locket pattern clasp which carries a motif similar to that on the Shako Plate. Across the left shoulder and supporting a pouch he wears a black patent leather Pouch Belt with bronze Lion Head Boss, Chain, Whistle and Whistle holder. The circular Pouch Belt Plate appears to be diestamped and carries the Dragon motif already described within a closed wreath of laurel. A black patent leather Sword Belt and Slings worn under the jacket supports a Sword and Scabbard of polished steel. The hilt and Guard of the Sword depicted resembles more the Cavalry pattern than the 1827 Rifle Regiment pattern most favoured by Rifle Volunteer Officers.

Athough Grey was the shade uniform generally favoured by the Rifle Volunteers of the County, the 7th (Conway) Corps was the exception. A photograph exists of a group of Volunteer Officers and N.C.O.s described as No.7 Section, 8th Volunteer Corps, School of Musketry, Hythe, dated July 1861. Included in this and a companion print is Sergeant Polin of the 7th (Conway) Corps, who is dressed in a very plain but practical uniform of Rifle Green.

HEAD-DRESS

Sergeant Polin is wearing a dark green Shako which resembles a similar form of head-dress authorised for wear by the Regular Army on the 28th November, 1860. It appears to have a black patent leather peak and is bound at the base of the headpiece with a band of similar material. It carries no ball tuft or plume decoration, and the blackened badge on the front, although not completely clear, incorporates the stringed Bugle Horn device so popular with Rifle Volunteers of that period.

UNIFORM

The Jacket or Tunic of dark green material is single breasted and is fastened at the front with eight black (probably horn or blackened brass) buttons. The Collar is faced with black material and the plain pointed cuffs are edged with black cord or tape. Single black shoulder cords and button embellish the shoulders, and the matching trousers have a black stripe down each outside leg seam.

ACCOUTREMENTS

A black patent leather belt with balck Ammunition Pouch and Bayonet Frog are worn around the waist.

Up to c.1865 the Badges worn by the seven individual Corps were different but, apart from the information already given, no further photographs or descriptions have been found.

At about that date, the Administrative Battalions being under pressure to standardise in matters of dress in many cases adopted the Scarlet Tunics and Blue Trousers similar to those worn by the Infantry of the Line, and the hitherto individual Corps Badges slowly gave way to a more standardised form. The Carnarvonshire Rifle Volunteers appear to have followed this line of action, and the reader will note that c.1865 a standard 'Carnarvonshire Rifle Volunteers' Waist Belt Clasp was in use by the Officers.

In 1873, the Shako went out of fashion with Rifle Regiments and a Busby, in Lambskin for Officers and in Sealskin for Other Ranks was taken into use. a similar pattern was also worn by the Royal Engineers. Some Rifle Volunteer Battalions also adopted this style of head-dress and a photograph of Sergeant Vague of the Bangor College Company, c.1879, shows head-dress of this pattern. Unfortunately the quality of the reproduced photograph does not allow one to identify the Insignia, and it is not certain whether its wear at that date extended throughout the Flintshire Administrative Battalion, or was confined solely to its Carnarvonshire elements. The former would appear to be most likely.

In 1878 the Home Service Pattern Helmet with spike fitting was introduced for wear by the Army. In due course the Helmet was also acquired by the Volunteer Corps, and can be found in Blue cloth, Dark Green or Grey with White Metal, Bronze or blackened fittings.

The shade worn by the 1st Flintshire and Carnarvonshire Rifle Volunteers during the period 1880-1884 was likely Blue, but it is interesting to note that the Carnarvonshire Companies wore a distinctive Helmet Plate which distinguished them from the Flintshire element. Such a Plate exists and takes the form of a white metal Maltese Cross surmounted with a blank plinth and the Victorian Crown. At its centre, the Plumes, Coronet and Motto of the Prince of Wales within a circle inscribed 'Carnarvon Rifle Volunteers' which anglicised spelling for the County is slightly incorrect. An example of the plate has also been seen in blackened brass.

The Army List of November 1880 describes the Uniform of the 1st Flintshire and Carnarvonshire Rifle Volunteers as Scarlet with Green Facings. This as applied to the Jacket or Tunic tells us that it had the collar and cuffs faced with green cloth. The Trousers were blue with the usual red stripe.

MAJOR G.S. DOUGLAS PENNANT —
1st ADMINISTRATIVE BN, CARNARVON RIFLE VOLUNTEERS, c.1861
From an original Painting
By kind permission of the R.W.F. Museum

8th VOLUNTEER COURSE, No.7 SECTION — SCHOOL OF MUSKETRY, HYTHE, c.1861.
SERGEANT E. POLIN, 7th (CONWAY) CORPS CAN BE SEEN IN THE FRONT RANK KNEELING, SECOND FROM RIGHT OF PICTURE.

Sgt.Inst. Curtis, Cpl. Tylor 13th Hants; Cpl. Thomas, 15th Shrop.; Capt. Sir W. Knighton, 12 Hants.; Capt. Richardson, 8th Hants.; Capt. Bostock, Staffs.

Lieut. Col. Vivian, 4th Glam.; Capt. Talbot, 1st Glam.; Sgt. E. Polin, 7 Carnarvon; Sgt. Evans, 2nd Radnor.

8th Volunteer Course, School of Musketry, Hythe, July, 1861 Sgt. Polin, 7th Carnarvonshire Corps stands with his Rifle at the 'Order' on the extreme left of the Group.

HELMET PLATE, c.1880. CARNARVONSHIRE RIFLE VOLUNTEERS.
WHITE METAL, BLACKENED OR SILVERED.
(Owen Collection)

H.M. Silver Officers Pouch Belt Plate
possibly that worn by the 7th (Conway) Corps,
Carnarvonshire Rifle Volunteers c.1862
By kind permission of H.L. King

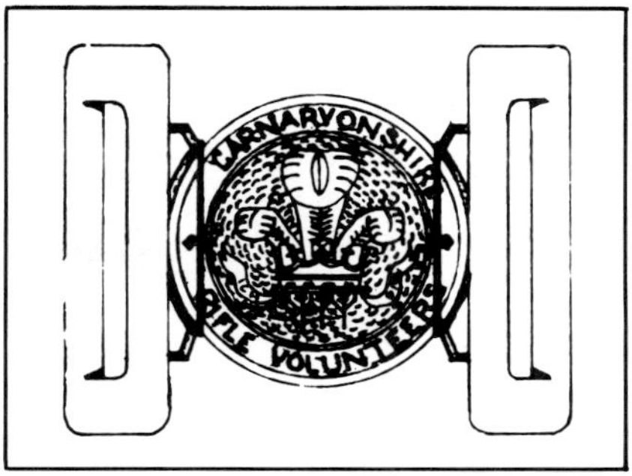

OTHER RANKS WAIST BELT CLASP
CARNARVONSHIRE RIFLE VOLUNTEERS c.1870
White Metal Construction

OFFICERS WAIST BELT CLASP
1st and 2nd (Penrhyn) Corps c.1862
Silver Plated

Clasp. Waist Belt. Officers Pattern. Carnarvonshire Rifle Volunteers c.1865
The whole in Silver plated Metal

(Owen Collection)

Sergeant Vague. Bangor College Company,
1st Administrative Battalion, Flintshire Rifle Volunteers, c.1879.
The Uniform Jacket is Scarlet with Green Facings and is worn with Blue Trousers with Red Stripe on each outside leg seam. The Plume on the Busby is likely Green. The Badge, a French Bugle Horn in blackened metal below a Cord Boss, the device on which can not be identified.
Courtesy: R. Westlake

VOLUNTEER BATTALIONS OF THE ROYAL WELSH FUSILIERS, 1884-1908

2nd VOLUNTEER BATTALION, ROYAL WELSH FUSILIERS, 1884-1897

The Cardwell Army reorganisation of 1881 converted Sub District No.23 of the Northern Military District into Regimental District No.23, Northern Command, and affiliated the Rifle Volunteer Corps to the Royal Welsh Fusiliers: in consequence, the 1st Denbigh, and 1st Flint and Carnarvon Rifle Volunteer Corps became Volunteer Battalions of that regiment. By General Order No.78 of June 1884 the link between the Volunteers and the Territorial Regiment was further strengthened when the 1st Flint and Carnarvon Corps was redesignated as the 2nd Volunteer Battalion, Royal Welsh Fusiliers with Caernarfonshire providing four Companies to the strength of the new Battalion. By 1897 that contribution had greatly increased, the County in that year providing more than half the strength to make up the 16 Companies of the Battalion.

3rd VOLUNTEER BATTALION, ROYAL WELSH FUSILIERS, 1897-1908

The substantial contribution made by Caernarfonshire to the strength of the 2nd Volunteer Battalion, Royal Welsh Fusiliers had by 1897 made it evident that the County was quite capable of supporting its own Volunteer Infantry Battalion. On the 26th May, a decision to that effect having been made, the establishment of the 2nd Volunteer Battalion was reduced to 8 Companies, and the Caernarvonshire contribution withdrawn to form, with Headquarters in Caernarfon, a new Battalion of 8 Companies styled 3rd Volunteer Battalion, Royal Welsh Fusiliers. The Battalion was included with the 1st and 2nd Volunteer Battalions, R.W.F.; Cheshire, Shropshire and Herefordshire Volunteer Battalions in the Welsh Border Brigade.

Battalion activities continued much the same as during past years, the Officers and Men assembling at regular intervals for training at their drill stations and proceeding once annually as a Battalion to Camp in places as far separated as Conway and Aldershot. During the Boer War 1899-1902 three Volunteer Service Companies were formed from the 1st, 2nd and 3rd Volunteer Battalions of the Royal Welsh Fusiliers which successively between 1900 and 1902 served with the 1st Bn. Royal Welsh Fusiliers on campaign in South

Africa. The 1st Volunteer Service Company joined 1. R.W.F. at Modder Spruit on March 12th, 1900, and commenced the first stage of the journey home on the 28th October, 1901. They were relieved by the 2nd Volunteer Service Company, and that in turn by the third — which last, on completion of a period of garrison duty on the Schoonspruit Railway commenced their return journey to the United Kingdom on June 13th, 1902. The 3rd Volunteer Battalion was represented in each of the above mentioned Service Companies, and lost as a result of disease or sickness the following men whose names are inscribed on the Regimental Memorial in Wrexham Parish Church. All appear to have been members of the 1st Volunteer Service Company.

7417 Sgt. C. Jones
Died in Capetown, 5th May, 1900
Awarded Queen's Medal with bar 'Natal'

7302 Pte. A. Deverill
Died at Kimberely, 8th May, 1900
Awarded the Queen's Medal with bar 'Natal'

7353 Pte. J. Lewis
Died at Sea, 21st May, 1901
Awarded the Queen's Medal with bar 'Natal'

7347 Pte. Norman Roberts
Died of Heart Disease, Krugersdorp, 16th August, 1900
Is also listed on the Boer War Memorial at Rhyl.

A Document preserved in the Archives of the Royal Welsh Fusiliers Museum, compiled, c.1904, by Mr R. Norris of Twthill Vaults, lists the men of Carnarvon town who served with the Volunteer Service Companies of the R.W.F. in South Africa. Listed are the following:

7306	Cpl. H. Vaughan	Thomas Street
7562	Lieut./Cpl. T. Lloyd	
7515	Lieut./Cpl. J. Heard	
7308	Pte. G. Jones	Balaklava Road
7309	Pte. W.G. Tilling	St. David's Road
7310	Pte. P.S. Evans	Fronalaw, Twthill
7311	Pte. J. Williams	North Penrallt
7312	Pte. H. Hughes	North Penrallt
7322	Pte. G. Williams	North Penrallt
7313	Pte. G. Langston	Poole Street
7523	Pte. T.D. Williams	
7524	Pte. R.W. Williams	
7561	Pte. R. Parry	Mount Street
7573	Pte. W.S. Evans	

The Records of the services of the Volunteer Battalions of the Royal Welsh Fusiliers held by the Regimental Museum in Caernarfon are, to say the least, sparse. Those interested in further information on their activities will find the contemporary issues of the North Wales Newspapers somewhat more fruitful ground. The Carnarvonshire Volunteer Battalion at home during the period 1899-1902 continued its normal training programme, but in 1900 saw Anglesey represented in its ranks on the formation of a Company with Drill Station at Holyhead.

In 1901, the Established Strength of the Battalion was 1,291, with an Enrolled Strength of 1,053 of which 1,040 were returned as 'Efficient'. The Battalion had a thriving Cyclist Detachment numbering 77 Other Ranks, and provided the majority in numbers of the 1,248 Volunteers then active in the County. Whilst on annual training under canvas at Scarborough in 1905, a dispute and disturbance over rations took place. It resulted in the dismissal from the Battalion of 26 men from the Holyhead Company for their involvement in that affair. One can imagine their complaint to have been similar to that described by Robert Graves in 'Goodbye to All That', when the soldier at the Wrexham Depot complaining about his Army breakfast shouted words similar to "Dim bacon, Dim Wyau, Dim bloody brecwast." (No Bacon, No Eggs, No bloody Breakfast)

In 1906, the Welsh Border Volunteer Infantry Brigade was reorganised and renamed North Wales Border Volunteer Infantry Brigade. This resulted in the withdrawl of the 3rd Volunteer Battalion from that organisation and its attachment for training purposes to the Mersey Volunteer Infantry Brigade which had its Headquarters in Wrexham.

In 1907 the Battalion fairly well distributed around the Country had Drill Stations at Carnarvon, Porthmadoc, Penygroes, Llanberis, Conway, Penmaenmawr, Pwllheli and Holyhead, at which stage its days as part of the Volunteer Force were numbered.

The Report of the War Office (Reconstitution) Committee, better known as the 'Esher Report' had been published successively in February and March 1904, and set in motion a series of necessary and far reaching changes which were to result in the death of the old style Volunteer Army. When Mr Haldane, the Liberal War Secretary, took office in 1906, many changes were already in hand, but it fell to him and others to see the whole through to a successful conclusion.

Reducing the three echelons of the Land Forces of the Crown (viz: Regular Army, Militia and Volunteer Force) to two, he created from the Regular Troops available in the United Kingdom an Expeditionary, or Field Force, which on paper at least, was to be in all respects ready for mobilisation on the outbreak of War. Basically it consisted of six Infantry Divisions and six Brigades of Cavalry together with supporting arms, the whole being ready for transportation at maximum speed to any point where it was required for action. In the background at home, the old Militia converted to a Special Reserve would provide the necessary reinforcement drafts, and the Volunteer Force, reformed on a much reduced form as the Territorial Force would be responsible for home defence and garrison work, and similar to the Militia of earlier years produce volunteers for active service with the Expeditionary Force abroad. That part of the change which applied to the Auxiliary Land Forces of the Crown became Law in the Territorial and Reserve Forces Act of 1907. At midnight, March 31st, 1908, the old Volunteer Force and hence 3rd Volunteer Battalion, Royal Welsh Fusiliers stood down, to be reborn on April 1st as the 6th (Carnarvonshire and Anglesey) Battalion, The Royal Welsh Fusiliers (T.F.). Established Strength for the new Battalion was set at 25 Officers, 863 Other Ranks — a figure not met until the outbreak of World War 1. Many of those who had served in the old Volunteer Battalion did not extend their services to the new, due mainly to the fact that the terms of service which were demanded from members of the Territorial Force were far more stringent and demanding.

On conversion, the Battalion was located as follows:

H.Q. and 'A' Company	Carnarvon
'B' Company	Porthmadoc
'C' Company	Penygroes with sub drill station at Nantlle
'D' Company	Llanberis with sub drill station at Ebenezer
'E' Company	Conway with sub drill station at Llandudno
'F' Company	Penmaenmawr
'G' Company	Pwllheli with sub drill station at Criccieth
'H' Company	Holyhead with sub drill station at Menai Bridge

The Battalion with other T.F. units formed part of the North Wales Infantry Brigade of the Welsh Division.

CARNARVONSHIRE RIFLE VOLUNTEERS & SUCCESSORS, 1860-1908

1860
1st, 2nd, 3rd, 4th, 5th, 6th & 7th
Corps formed

1860
August 2nd
1st Administrative Battalion
Carnarvonshire Rifle Volunteers
formed

1865
6th (Bangor) Corps disbanded

1866
7th (Conway) Corps disbanded

1874
1st, 2nd, 3rd, 4th, 5th Corps
Carnarvonshire Rifle Vols.
united with
1st Admin. Bn. Flintshire
Rifle Volunteers

1875
1st Corps disbanded

1877
2nd and 5th Corps disbanded

1878
5th (Llanberis) Corps formed

1880
1st Flintshire & Carnarvonshire
Rifle Volunteer Corps formed
'G', 'H', 'I' & 'K' Carnarvonshire Companies

1884
2nd Volunteer Battalion
Royal Welsh Fusiliers formed
4 Carnarvonshire Companies

1897
3rd Volunteer Battalion
Royal Welsh Fusiliers formed
8 Companies. HQ: Carnarfon

1908
6th (Carnarvonshire and Anglesey)
Bn, Royal Welsh Fusiliers (T.F.)

CARNARVONSHIRE FIELD AND COMPANY OFFICERS AND OTHERS SERVING WITH THE 2nd VOLUNTEER BATTALION, ROYAL WELSH FUSILIERS — DECEMBER 1896

Hon. Colonel, The Marquis of Anglesey
Lieut. Colonel C.H. Rees
Captain A.T.A. Sarson
Captain H.J. Roberts (Inst. of Musketry)
Lieut. J. Williams
Lieut. W.H. Lloyd-Griffiths
2nd Lieut. R.R. Williams
2nd Lieut. W.F. Russell
2nd Lieut. A.W. Menzies
2nd Lieut. E.J. Owen
Q.M. T.B. Farrington
Surgeon Captain R.A. Pritchard
Surgeon Captain W.J. Morris
Surgeon Captain T.L.K. Davies
Surgeon Lieut. E.T. Hughes
A/Chaplain Rev. T. Edwards
A/Chaplain Rev. L.R. Hughes, M.A.

3rd VOLUNTEER BATTALION, ROYAL WELSH FUSILIERS

List of Officers (Monthly Army List May 1898)
Headquarters: Carnarvon
Uniform: Scarlet   Facings: Blue

Hon. Colonel, The Marquis of Anglesey		13 May, 1891
Lieut. Colonel C.H. Rees, V.D.		17 April, 1895
	Command of Battalion	26 May, 1897
Major G.R. Ashley		3 February, 1897
Major O. Thomas		9 February, 1898
Captain A.T.A. Sarson		
Captain H.J. Roberts		
Captain R.H.M. Roberts		
Captain W.H. Edwards		
Captain C.T. Allard		
Captain J. Williams		
Captain J.R. Pritchard		
Lieut. W.D. Henderson		
Lieut. A.W. Jones		Captain & Adjutant

Lieut. H.R. Maxted
Lieut. W. Lloyd Griffith
Lieut. R.R. Williams
2nd Lieut. W.R. Russel
2nd Lieut. A.W. Menzies
2nd Lieut. E.J. Owen
2nd Lieut. S. Smith-Twort
2nd Lieut. W.B. Hunter
2nd Lieut. J.R.W. Blake

H.H. Were
Quartermaster T. Farrington

Medical Officers
Surgeon Captain R. Pritchard
Surgeon Captain W.J. Morris
Surgeon Captain T.L. Davies
Surgeon Captain F.T. Hughes

Acting Chaplains
R. Edwards
R. Hughes

List of Officers (Army List September 1900)
Headquarters: Carnarvon
Uniform: Scarlet Facings: Blue

Hon. Colonel J.E. Greaves	16 November, 1898
Lieut. Colonel & Hon. Colonel C.H. Rees, V.D.	17 April, 1895
Major A.T.A. Sarson	4 April, 1900
Major H.J. Roberts (Inst. of Musketry)	14 July, 1900
Captain R.H.M. Roberts	3 June, 1986
Captain W.H. Edwards	3 June, 1896
Captain C.T. Allard	3 February, 1897
Captain J. Williams	2 April, 1898
Captain J.R. Pritchard	16 April, 1898
Captain C.H. Darbishire	25 April, 1900
Captain E. Freeman	13 June, 1900
Captain W.E. Darbishire	14 July, 1900
Captain W.H. Lloyd Griffith	24 July, 1900
Lieut. R.R. Williams	2 April, 1898
Lieut. E.J. Owen	3 September, 1898
Lieut. W.B.H. Hunter	14 March, 1900
Lieut. J.R.W. Blake	20 June, 1900
Lieut. E.B. Booker	24 July, 1900
2nd Lieut. H.T. Jenkins	2 May, 1900

2nd Lieut. J.R. Williams	2 May, 1900
2nd Lieut. W.A. Tuxford	2 May, 1900
2nd Lieut. A. Bremner	23 May, 1900
2nd Lieut. W.A. Hughes	24 May, 1900
2nd Lieut. A. Ivor Parry	24 May, 1900
2nd Lieut. G.W. Kinman	18 July, 1900
2nd Lieut. J. Evans	18 July, 1900
2nd Lieut. R.G. Jones	18 July, 1900
Captain & Adjutant H.H. Were	Appt. 1 July, 1896
Quartermaster T. Armstrong	2 May, 1900
Surgeon Captain R.A. Prichard	17 August, 1881
Surgeon Captain W.J. Morris	15 March, 1890
Surgeon Captain T.L.K. Davies, M.B.	7 October,1896
Surgeon Lieut. E.T. Hughes	20 May, 1896
A/Chaplain Rev. T. Edwards	2 February, 1894
A/Chaplain Rev. L.R. Hughes, M.A.	17 July, 1895
A/Chaplain J. Jenkins, B.A.	11 April, 1900

List of Officers (Army List February 1908)
Headquarters: Carnarvon
Uniform: Scarlet Facings: Blue
Battle Honours: South Africa 1900-02

Hon. Colonel J.E. Greaves	16 November, 1898
Lieut. Colonel C.H. Darbishire	28 May, 1904
Major H.J. Roberts	14 July, 1900
Major R.H.M. Roberts. C.M.G.	27 August, 1904
Captain W.A. Tuxford (Inst. of Musketry)	14 December, 1901
Captain A.H. Wheeler	19 March, 1904
Captain H.T. Jenkins	28 May, 1904
Captain A.E.R. Jelf-Reveley	6 August, 1904
Captain O.H.M. Williams	3 May, 1905
Captain J. Evans	23 December, 1905
Captain R. Griffith	10 January, 1906
Captain J.H. Addie	11 November, 1906
Captain G. Drage	10 June, 1907
Lieut. E.B. Booker	24 July, 1900
Lieut. H.W. Darbishire	30 July, 1904
Lieut. G.L. Battersby	8 September, 1906
Lieut. C.W. Darbishire	8 September, 1906
Lieut. E. Andrews	8 September, 1906
2nd Lieut. A.S. Lewis	7 June, 1907
2nd Lieut. G.L. O'Conner	7 June, 1907
Hon. Lieut. and Quartermaster T. Armstrong	2 May, 1900

Surgeon Major T.L.K. Davies, M.B.	8 November, 1907
Surgeon Captain John R. Williams	13 August, 1904
A/Chaplain Rev. T. Edwards	3 February, 1894
A/Chaplain Rev. L.R. Hughes, M.A.	17 July, 1895
A/Chaplain Rev. E.B. Thomas, B.A.	15 May, 1901
A/Chaplain Rev. R.L. Roberts, M.A.	4 August, 1906

UNIFORM, BADGES AND INSIGNIA 2nd and 3rd VOLUNTEER BATTALIONS, THE ROYAL WELSH FUSILIERS

On becoming an element of, and finally a Volunteer Battalion of, the Royal Welsh Fusiliers, the Uniform Dress of that regiment, Scarlet with Blue Facings with appropriate Volunteer designations was adopted. In Undress however, some Officers according to contemporary photographs appear wearing a dark blue frogged tunic similar to that worn by Rifle Regiments whilst others c.1892 appear in the Infantry style Blue Frock. The Head-dress for everyday use c.1892 appears mainly to be the blue cloth Undress Forage Cap (sometimes referred to as the Station Master pattern) with silver braided patent leather peak, black laced headband and silver embroidered regimental pattern grenade on the front. A blue Torin Field Service Cap with silver piping and displaying a similar silver embroidered Grenade was also worn. The Rifle Volunteer custom of wearing a Pouch Belt Plate, continued, and examples of the rather handsome patterns worn by the Officers and Senior N.C.O.s of both 2nd and 3rd Volunteer Battalions are included amongst accompanying illustrations. Distinctive Waist Belt Clasps were also worn by Officers of both Battalions, but Other Ranks wore a white metal version of the General Service or Universal pattern.

In Full Dress, a Private of the 3rd Volunteer Battalion, c.1898, would be dressed as follows:

HEAD-DRESS

A black Racoon-skin Cap approx 9″ high at the front with a chin chain of burnished or plated white metal backed with black leather. On the front a diestamped white metal Grenade having on the ball, the motif of the Plumes, Coronet and Motto of the Prince of Wales.

UNIFORM

A Tunic of Scarlet cloth with blue collar and rounded blue cuffs singlebreasted and fastened with seven white metal buttons of the general service pattern at the front. Shoulder Straps were blue and edged in white piping as was also the upper edge of the collar and leading edge of the tunic. The Shoulder Straps carried the white embroidered designation 3/V/Grenade/W.F., one above the other and in that order. On the collar small white metal grenades with plain ball were displayed, one on each side, flames outwards.

A white buff leather belt with white metal Universal Waist Belt Clasp Frog. Trousers of Blue Cloth with a red stripe down each outside leg seam and black polished ankle boots completed the outfit.

2nd LIEUT. OWEN THOMAS, 2nd V.B. ROYAL WELSH FUSILIERS
LATER MAJOR, 3rd V.B. ROYAL WELSH FUSILIERS
By kind permission of R. Westlake

Officers Group and Battalion Goat, 2nd Volunteer Battalion
The Royal Welsh Fusiliers — Valley Camp, Anglesey, 1892.
Lieut. Owen Thomas, centre, is identified by a 'X'
By kind permission of R. Westlake

3rd Volunteer Battalion, Officers and N.C.O.s Group c.1898.
The Dress of the Cyclist Sergeant is of particular interest as in his Machine.
By kind permission of Gwynedd Archives Service

Typical of the Annual Camps under canvas enjoyed by the Volunteers in the 1890s
Owen Collection

A Signals Sergeant, 2nd Volunteer Bn, Royal Welsh Fusiliers with Heliograph and Signalling Lamp. c.1898
(R.W.F. Archives)

Non Commissioned Officers, 2nd Volunteer Bn, Royal Welsh Fusiliers
in Full Dress, c.1898
(R.W.F. Archives)

Non Commissioned Officers of the 3rd Volunteer Bn, Royal Welsh Fusiliers
Permanent Staff, c.1898
(R.W.F. Archives)

Permanent Staff and Volunteer Non Commissioned Officers 2nd Volunteer Battalion, Royal Welsh Fusiliers, c.1898
(R.W.F. Archives)

Non Commissioned Officers, 3rd Volunteer Bn, Royal Welsh Fusiliers, c.1898, including a Drum Major and Colour Sergeant.
(R.W.F. Museum Archives)

An Officer, N.C.O. Group, 2nd Volunteer Bn, Royal Welsh Fusiliers c.1898. Included, the Sergeant Major, a Hospital Sergeant of the Battalion Bearer Section and a Band Sergeant.
(R.W.F. Archives)

Group. 3rd Volunteer Battalion, Royal Welsh Fusiliers with the Battalion Goat, c.1902

By kind permission of Gwynedd Archives Service

WAIST BELT CLASP. OFFICERS PATTERN
2nd VOLUNTEER BATTALION, ROYAL WELSH FUSILIERS, c.1887
Silver Plated Metal

The 1st and 3rd Volunteer Battalions wore a similar pattern clasp with appropriate Battalion designations.
Owen Collection

Pouch Belt Plate — Officers S/P Pattern —2nd V.B. Royal Welsh Fusiliers c. 1890
A silver plated Pouch Belt Plate of this Pattern was worn by all Volunteer Battalions of the Royal Welsh Fusiliers with appropriate title scrolls.

Other Ranks Shoulder Strap, 2nd Volunteer Bn, Royal Welsh Fusiliers.
Black embroidered designations on a red cloth ground.

Owen Collection

Grenade Badges. Volunteer Battalions. Royal Welsh Fusiliers
Left. Officers Fur Cap Grenade. Silver Plated. c.1900
Centre. Glengarry Cap Badge. Other Ranks. c.1887. White Metal
Right. Racoon Skin Cap Grenade. Other Ranks. White Metal. c.1900
Owen Collection

Top. Officers Silver Plated Pouch Belt Plate. 3rd Volunteer Bn. R.W.F. c.1900 a similar pattern was worn by Officers of the 2nd Volunteer Battalion during the same period.

Bottom. Cap. Badge. Other Ranks. 3rd Volunteer Bn, R.W.F. c.1900 also found in Gilding Metal.

Owen Collection

THE ANGLESEY TROOP (Beaumaris and Amlwch) DENBIGHSHIRE HUSSARS YEOMANRY, 1901-1908

The services of this troop are recorded under 'C' (CARNARVONSHIRE SQUADRON, DENBIGHSHIRE HUSSARS.

'C' (CARNARVONSHIRE) SQUADRON, DENBIGHSHIRE HUSSARS, 1901-1908

Although attempts had been made in 1795 and 1819 to raise a Corps of Yeomanry Cavalry in the County, Caernarfonshire was not represented in the Yeomanry Force until 1885, when due to the efforts of Captain Sydney Platt, a few men from the County were recruited for the Denbighshire Hussars.

The reverses suffered during the first few months of the South African (Boer) War of 1899-1902 caused H.M. Government to realise the value of Mounted Infantry and to set up a Committee to consider a reorganisation of the Yeomanry Force, and to recommend ways and means of making it better suited to meet the demands of warfare in that day and age.

The recommendations of that Committee were incorporated in the Militia and Auxiliary Forces Act of April 1901, which legislation together with Army Order 109/1901 resulted in many changes. As a result the Denbighshire Hussars were redesignated as the Denbighshire Hussars Imperial Yeomanry, almost trebled in strength, and was to be organised as 4 Squadrons. The increase in strength allowed the allocation to Caernarfonshire of one Squadron of the regiment. Designated 'C' (CARNARVONSHIRE) SQUADRON, it was raised by Captain Eric Platt, and included a Troop drawn from the Island of Anglesey.

Annual Training under the new rules was to amount to 16 days, of which period each Yeoman had to complete 14 clear days in camp to qualify as efficient. During Camp, the Officers were paid rates equivalent to their rank in the Regular Army. Other Ranks were paid daily rates as follows:

Regimental Sergeant Major	9s 6d
Regimental Quartermaster Sergeant	8s 2d
Squadron Sergeant Major	8s 2d
Squadron Quartermaster Sergeant	8s 2d

Corporals	7s 6d
Trumpeters	5s 8d
Private	5s 6d

and any rank providing his own Horse for Camp received an additional £5 Allowance for the period.

Rifles, Bayonets and Saddlery were supplied from Government sources, but Khaki Clothing and Spurs had to be provided by the regiment out of its Contingency Allowance. In addition to the minimum 14 day attendance at Camp, Yeomen were also required to attend at least 6 (Recruits 12) Troop or Squadron Drills annually, and to obtain not less than Second Class Standard in Musketry.

The Squadron was represented (although not at full strength) at the 1901 annual camp at Wynnstay near Ruabon, and by May 9th, 1902 was sufficiently organised and trained to be able to undertake its first public duty by providing the Mounted Escorts required on the occasion of the visit of their Royal Highnesses, the Prince and Princess of Wales, to the County. Appreciation of its services on that occasion was expressed in a letter from the Royal Household to the General Officer Commanding the North Western District.

"By direction of the Prince of Wales, I have the honour to request that you will be good enough to convey to the Officers commanding the following Corps the expression of His Royal Highness's satisfaction with the manner in which they respectively performed their duties of furnishing escorts, Guards of Honour, or when lining the streets during the visit of their Royal Highnesses to Bangor, Carnarvon, Dinorwic Quarries and Rhyl on the 8th, 9th, 10th and 12th instants. His Royal Highness was much pleased with the appearance of the Troops under Arms."

On May 27th, 1902, the Squadron joined the regiment under the command of Lieut. Colonel Parry for annual training at Denbigh. The 1903 Camp was held at Kerry, Mongomeryshire, where the regiment assembled on May 12th. 'C' Squadron (Headquarters — Bangor) was still under the command of Captain Platt, and its Troop locations at that date were:

No.1	Bangor
No.2	Anglesey (Beaumaris and Amlwch)
No.3	Caernarfon and Llandudno
No.4	Porthmadoc and Llanrwst

Annual Camp in 1904 was held at Llanfairfechan commencing May 26th during which the Inspecting Officer commented favourably on the organisation and achievements of the regiment since reorganisation.

During that year also, 'C' Squadron was represented at the ceremony held in Caernarfon to unveil the South Africa Memorial to those of the County who had lost their lives in the Boer War.

Venue for Camp in 1905 was St. Asaph where the regiment assembled on May 25th. In 1906 it joined the Glamorgan Imperial Yeomanry in

Llangammarch Wells, but inclement weather and an unsuitable Camping Ground resulted in the major part of that training being completed at Margam Park, Glamorgan. There the Carnarvonshire Squadron had the satisfaction of winning the Regimental Challenge Cup.

In 1907 the Camp was held at Denbigh, and during the month which followed 'C' Squadron provided a travelling escort for the King on the occasion of his visit to Bangor on July 9th.

The year saw the designation 'Imperial' dropped from the Regimental Title.

On April 1st, 1908, the Denbighshire Yeomanry and hence the Carnarvonshire Squadron became part of the new Territorial Force. Its history at that stage was far from ended, but can be followed by reference to the history of the parent regiment.

UNIFORM DRESS AND INSIGNIA, c.1905

The Full Dress Uniform was very similar to that worn by the New South Wales Lancers during the same period. The Head-dress consisted of a drab felt Bush Hat with red pagri and white feather hackle. The left side was turned up and displayed the regimental Cap Badge. The tunic of drab cloth was double breasted with scarlet collar, and scarlet shoulder straps bearing the brass title D.H.I.Y. For full dress a scarlet plastron displaying two rows of silver regimental buttons was worn with a scarlet and yellow Lancer Girdle. Officers wore much the same kit but added gold Shoulder Straps and a Scarlet and Gold Lancer Girdle as well as Gold and Scarlet Sword Belts and Slings.

Breeches were made of drab cloth or Bedford Cord and were worn with drab putties and spurs of the hunting pattern. Officers wore Wellington Boots and Box Spurs and in dismounted order, drab Overalls with single scarlet stripe. Saddlery was of the Colonial Pattern. No Sheepskins or Throat Plumes were worn on the Horse Furniture.

The Yeoman depicted seated wears the form of dress described with the exception of his Lancer Girdle. The Regimental pattern Collar Badges can be clearly seen as also the Austrian Knot of brown cord on the cuffs.

The Cap Badge worn by Other Ranks sealed 23rd October, 1901, consisted of the Plumes, Coronet and Motto of the Prince of Wales in brass or gilding metal. The Collar Badges of similar size but with Plumes and Motto Scroll in White Metal and Coronet gilding metal together with the Shoulder Titles D.H.I.Y. were sealed 7th October, 1902. The Officers Cap Badge was similar but had added below a Scroll inscribed 'Denbighshire Hussars'. It comes in several verisons, i.e., the whole in gilding metal, with Plumes and Motto Scroll silver, Coronet and Title Scroll Gilt. Another similar with Coronet silver, and post 1906, the whole bronzed or brown painted.

For ordinary wear a Field Service Cap, drab with scarlet piping was worn which carried the appropriate Cap Badge. Officers also wore in Undress a drab leather peaked Forage Cap of Staff pattern with scarlet crown and headband.

It is unlikely that Other Ranks of the Carnarvonshire Squadron were in possession of the old Hussar Full Dress.

AN OFFICER OF THE DENBIGHSHIRE HUSSARS IMPERIAL YEOMANRY c.1904

From an original Simkin Watercolour and by kind permission of J. Carey Hughes

A PRIVATE — DENBIGHSHIRE HUSSARS IMPERIAL YEOMANRY,
c.1904
By kind permission of C. Lewis

WAR OFFICE SEALED PATTERNS OF THE OTHER RANKS CAP AND COLLAR BADGES OF THE DENBIGHSHIRE HUSSARS IMPERIAL YEOMANRY. THE PLUMES, CORONET AND MOTTO SCROLL OF THE CAP AND COLLAR BADGES ARE IN WHITE METAL, AND THE CORONET IN BRASS/GILDING METAL
THE SHOULDER TITLES, BRASS.
THE LEFT HAND CARD IS DATED 23rd OCTOBER, 1901, AND THE RIGHT, 7th OCTOBER, 1902
By kind permission of K. Hook

CAP BADGE. DENBIGHSHIRE HUSSARS YEOMANRY
c.1908
(Dr J. Carey Hughes)

CONCLUSION

The year 1908 was a turning point in the history of the Militia and Auxiliary Forces generally, and provides a suitable date on which to close this account of the contribution made over 146 years by the Civilian Soldiers of Anglesey and Caernarfonshire. Their continuing story over 80 years to the present day is equally, if not more impressive, and deserves (hopefully within the present century) to be the subject for a similar Volume.

‘C’ SQUADRON PERSONALITIES KERRY CAMP, MONTGOMERYSHIRE.
1903
By kind permission of Gwynedd Archives Service

REFERENCE SOURCES AND BIBLIOGRAPHY

ANGLESEY MILITIA

PAINTINGS, PRINTS, DRAWINGS AND PHOTOGRAPHS

Engraving. Coloured.
Anglesey Militiamen (undated, but before c.1780)
Anon, The Militiaman — Plate 3.
See *Index to Military Costume Prints, 1500-1914* — AMOT 1972

Plate. Coloured
Anglesey Militiaman, c.1780
Appears in *A Collection of Coloured Plates — Uniforms of the various Militia Regiments* by John Osborne, Colonel of the Bedfordshire Regiment of Militia.
See also Article — *Militia Uniforms* by W.Y. Carman

ARCHIVAL AND BIBLIOGRAPHICAL SOURCES

Gwynedd Records Office — Llangefni (Anglesey) Office
Militia Documents — Uncatalogued
Box 1 and Box 2
Account of County Treasurer re the maintenance of the Families of Militiamen (late 18th/early 19th C)

Box 3

1. Treasurer's Accounts of Money paid to Wives of Men serving in the Anglesey Militia 1793-1816
2. Treasurer's Accounts of Money spent on Postage in connection with Men serving in the Militia where the families lived outside the County 1803-16
3. Treasurer's Accounts with Treasurers of other Counties re support of the Families of Militiamen 1793-1812
4. Lists of Men liable to serve in the Militia 1810, 1811, 1823, 1825.
5. Lists of all Men actually serving in the Militia in Active Service with Families to be maintained (no dates)
6. Return of Commissioned Officers c.1869
7. Treasurer's Vouchers of Money paid to Overseas of the Poor for the maintenance of the Families of Militiamen 1793-1811
8. Militia Stores and Barracks 1854-1879

9. Letters from War Office enclosing payment for the Accommodation of the Permanent Staff 1870-79
10. Papers re Money owed to Mr Sparrow, Adjutant of the Anglesey Militia, 1800-04
11. Miscellaneous File re Militia 1796-1878
12. Payments made by Overseas to Families of Militia men 1781-83, 1811-12
13. Lieutenancy (a) Qualification Roll 1787
    (b) Miscellaneous File re Lieutenancy 1846-77

PUBLIC RECORD OFFICE

PRO information for Anglesey Militia is listed under that of the Carnarvon Militia

Anglesey Militia
Note 1128. *Journal of the Society for Army Historical Research*
Vol. XXXII. No.132. Winter 1954

Anglesea Militia
Note 1683. *Journal of the Society for Army Historical Research*
Vol. LV. No.221. Spring 1977

Anglesea Militia — Memoirs of Herbert Jones.
Copy in Cardiff Central Library

Fenwick Copy Letter Book — National Library of Wales, Aberystwyth

The Constitutional Force — Colonel Jackson Hayes, C.B., C.M.G.

The County Fencibles and Militia Augmentation of 1794 (H.O. 50/31)
Article — *Journal of the Society for Army Historical Reserarch*
Vol. LV. No.221. Spring 1977

Welsh Militia Regiments 1757-1881, Their Badges and Buttons Article — Journal of the Society for Army Historical Research
Major H.G. Parkyn, OBE. Vol. XXXII. No.130. Summer 1954

Militia Uniforms
Article by W.Y. Carman
Jounral of the Society for Army Historical Research
Vol. XXXVI, No.147, September 1958

CARNARVONSHIRE MILITIA

PAINTINGS, PRINTS, DRAWINGS AND PHOTOGRAPHY

Engraving. Coloured
Carnarvonshire Militiaman (undated, but before c.1780)
Anon, The Militiaman — Plate II
See Index to *Military Costume Prints*, 1500-1914. AMOT 1972

Plate. Coloured
Carnarvonshire Militiaman. c.1780
Included in *A collection of Coloured Plates — Uniforms of the various Militia Regiments* by John Osborne, Colonel of the Bedfordshire Militia
See also Article — *Militia Uniforms* by W.Y. Carman

ARCHIVAL AND BIBLIOGRAPHICAL SOURCES

List of Officers, Correspondence and Papers, Carnarvonshire Militia and Others 1760-1986.
Clwyd Records Office. D/GA/1088-1096

Fenwick Copy Letter Book
National Library of Wales

Records. 4th Battalion, Royal Welsh Fusiliers
Museum of The Royal Welch Fusiliers, Caernarfon.

A History of Carnarvonshire 1294-1900, A.H. Dodd

The Society of Fort Williamsburg
Article. E.A. Jones, M.A., F.S.A., Y Cymmrodor. Vol. XLIV. 1935.

Welsh Militia Regiments 1757-1881
Article. Major H.G. Parkyn, OBE.
Journal of the Society for Army Historical Research
Vol. XXXII. No.130. Summer 1954.

Contemporary Newspapers including
The North Wales Gazette. The North Wales Chronicle. The Cambrian, The Hereford Journal and the *Gloucester Journal.*

Gwynedd County Archives Service (Caernarfon Office)
The Lieutenancy Papers (Militia Records) contain much useful information regarding the County Militia for the period 1796 to 1860. They include Orders and Correspondence for the various County Sub-Divisions, General Correspondence relating to the County Militia, Monthly Returns, Returns of Strength, Lists of Militia Officers. The Poole Papers and Quarter Sessions Records are also the source for much related material.

X/Poole/43 for example is a Return of Men serving in the County Militia on the 27th July, 1813.

PUBLIC RECORDS OFFICE
Although many of the Militia Records which have survived are preserved locally, e.g., Quarter Sessions Records, Lieutenancy Papers and Private Family Manuscripts held by County Records Offices, the following are available for public search at the P.R.O. Kew. They contain information relating to the Militia Regiments of Anglesey and Caernarfonshire.

H.O.50. Appointment of Officers to the Militia, mid 18th to mid 19th centuries
H.O.51. Entry Books related to Records contained under H.O.50.
W.O.23/89-92. Registers of Pensions paid to Militia Officers 1868-92.
W.O.13. Muster Books and Pay Lists. Militia, from 1780.
E.182. Record of Payments to the Families of those who served in the embodied regiments during the Napoleonic Wars.
W.O.96. Attestation Forms. Other Ranks, Militia, 1806-1915 (but mainly second half 19th Century).
W.O.68. Miscellaneous Militia Records, including Order Books, Succession Books, Enrolment Books and Records of the service of Officers.

PROVISIONAL CAVALRY

PAINTINGS, PRINTS, DRAWINGS

None found.

ARCHIVAL AND BIBLIOGRAPHICAL SOURCES

Gwynedd Area Records — Caernarfon Office
Poole Papers, Vol.1 (1784-1820) include material relating to the raising of Provisional Cavalry in the County of Caernarfonshire. The Lieutenancy Papers held in the same Office include Copies and Schedules of the Cavalry Acts, the Minute Book of Meetings of the Lieutenancy in relation to same, Returns of the numbers of Horses available, and a List of the men enrolled.

History of the British Army, Vol.IV. Hon. J.W. Fortescue.
Macmillan & Co., London 1921

Provisional Cavalry 1797-1800. Article
Journal of the Society for Army Historical Research,
Vol XXXI, No.128, Winter 1953.

Public Record Office.
Provisional Cavalry — Formation, Disbandment, etc, of Corps, 1796-99
W.O.1/942. H.O.513151.

VOLUNTEERS 1794-1808

Archival and Bibliographical Sources
Willson's Volunteer Chart
included in an Article, *The Volunteer Army of Great Britain 1806*
by The Marquess of Cambridge, GCVO. *Journal of the Society for Army Historical Research.* Vol.XXXI. No's 127 and 128

The County Lieutenancies and the Army, J.W. Fortescue MacMillan & Co, 1909

The Volunteer Force 1803-04. Article by P.J. Haythornthwaite Journal of the Society for Army Historical Research. Vol.LXIV. No.260
The Historical of the British Army, Hon. J.W. Fortescue. Macmillan & Co., 1906
The Defenders. G. Cousins, Frederick Muller, London, 1968.
The Cambrian — National Library of Wales & Cardiff Central Library
The North Wales Gazette — National Library of Wales & Cardiff Central Library

Public Records Office
W.O. 34/155. Offers of Cities and Boroughs to raise Volunteer Corps in National Emergency, 1799.
W.O. 4/158 (105.106) Volunteer Formations, 1793-1795
W.O. 2/1. Lists of Corps and index to correspondence concerning same 1794-1796
W.O.40/10. Returns of various Volunteer Regiments, 1795-98
H.O.51/151-157. Formations, Establishments. Volunteer Corps. 1796-1806
H.O.50/458. Lists of Corps, 1797.
W.O.6/199. Formation, Conditions of Service. Pay and Allowances, Correspondence in connection with. 1798-1799
W.O.6/197-202. Formation. Continuation of Services of. Instructions as to. 1798-1803

CAERNARFONSHIRE RECORD OFFICE
The Poole Papers (see Catalogue Poole Papers, vol.1) contain references to the activities of Volunteer Corps of the County of Caernarfon for the period 1798-1808.

LOCAL MILITIA

PAINTINGS, PRINTS AND DRAWINGS

None found

ARCHIVAL AND BIBLIOGRAPHICAL SOURCES

Gwynedd Area Records — Caernarfon Office

Information relating to Local Militia may be found in the Lieutenancy Papers and the Poole Papers (see Catalogue of Vol.1). In the latter, for example, 40-1813 is a Copy List of Men enrolled in the Local Militia for the County of Carnarvon. Documents relating to the Local Milita in the Poole Records are not under that specific heading, but are included with material relating to the Militia and Auxiliary Forces of the County generally.

The Manual of Military Law, 1914.
The County Lieutenancies and the Army, 1803-14. J.W. Fortescue, MacMillan & Co., 1909.
History of the British Army, Vol.VI. Chap. XIX. Hon. J.W. Fortescue. MacMillan & Co. 1921
List of Officers of the Local Militia of Great Britain. War Office, 1810.
The North Wales Gazette 1808-16
The Cambrian 1808-16

ARTILLERY VOLUNTEERS — ANGLESEY AND CAERNARFONSHIRE

ARCHIVAL SOURCES

National Library of Wales — Porthmadoc MSS

Carnarvonshire Artillery Volunteers

678. Muster Roll.1st Carnarvonshire Artillery Volunteers, 1862

679/88. Nominal Rolls 1st Carnarvon Artillery Volunteers, 1878/79

692. Nominal Roll by Batteries of persons enrolled in the Bangor Company, 1st Cheshire and Carnarvon Artillery Volunteers, 1881.

694. Nominal Roll by Batteries of persons enrolled in the 1st Cheshire and Carnarvon Artillery Volunteer Corps, 1882-83.

BIBLIOGRAPHICAL

The Volunteer Artillery 1859-1908. N. Litchfield & R. Westlake Sherwood Press, Nottingham, 1982

Head-dress Badges of the British Army. A.L. Kipling & H.L. King Frederick Muller Ltd, 1972

Monthly Army Lists 1860-1908

North Wales Chronicle and other Regional Newspapers 1860-1908

RIFLE VOLUNTEERS 1860-1884

ARCHIVAL SOURCES CAERNARVONSHIRE RIFLE VOLUNTEERS

Porthmadoc MSS and Papers. National Library of Wales

614. Muster Roll 1st Company 1860
615-620. Nominal Roll 1st Company, 1864/65, 1869/70, 1872/73
621. Muster Roll 2nd Company, 1860
622-627. Nominal Roll, 2nd Company, 1863/65, 1869/70, 1872/73
628. Muster Roll, 3rd Company, 1860
629. Abstract of Muster Roll, 3rd Company, 1861
630-640. Nominal Roll, 3rd Company, 1864/65, 1869/70, 1872/78
641. Muster Roll, 4th Company, 1860
642-653. Nominal Roll, 4th Company, 1864/65, 1869, 1870, 1872/79
654-55. Muster Roll, 5th Company, 1860
656. Abstract of Muster Roll, 5th Company, 1861
657-64. Nominal Roll, 5th Company, 1864, 1869/70, 1872/73, 1876, 1879
665.67. Muster Roll, 6th Company, 1860
668-70. Muster Roll, 7th Company, 1860
671. Regimental Roll, 7th Company, 1860
672. Nominal Roll, Carnarvonshire Rifle Volunteer Corps, 1879
673. Nominal Roll Carnarvonshire Rifle Volunteer Corps, 1883
674. Roll of Officers, Carnarvon Rifle Volunteer Corps, 1861
675-76. Return from Nominal Roll, Carnarvon Rifle Volunteer Corps 1869/70
677. Letter approving appointment of G. Sholto Douglas Pennant as Major Commanding Rifle Volunteer Corps in Caernarfonshire W.O. dated 27 February, 1860
691. Muster Roll, 1st Company, Penrhyn Rifle Volunteers, 1860
693. Nominal Roll by Companies of 1st Flint and Carnarvon Rifle Volunteer Corps, 1881/82

VOLUNTEER BATTALIONS.
ROYAL WELSH FUSILIERS — 1884-1908

ARCHIVAL SOURCES

Commission
E. Bremner, 3rd Volunteer Bn, R.W.F.
1915. Arch. R7/4.L/d. R.W.F. Museum

Commission.
H. Webb-Bowen, 3rd Volunteer Bn, R.W.F.
1916. Arch. R7/4.L/d. R.W.F. Museum

Letters and Accounts. 2nd Volunteer Bn, R.W.F.
re Division of Funds on separation of the Carnarvonshire
Companies in 1897 2601. Arch. R15/2.L/d. R.W.F. Museum

Album. 2nd Volunteer Bn, R.W.F. and Successors, 1897-1935
2927. Arch./Lib.L/ph. R.W.F. Mueseum

North Wales Newspapers 1880-1908 various
National Library of Wales
British Library

Bibliographical Sources

Regimental Records of the Royal Welsh Fusiliers
Cary and McCance

Monthly Army Lists 1881-1908
London Gazette 1881-1908
The Volunteer Services Magazine 1892-1898
The Territorial Year Book No.1, 1909
The Rifle Volunteers. R. Westlake. Picton Publishing 1982
Lineage Book of the British Army. 1660-1968. J.B.M. Frederick.
Hope Farm Press. Cornwallville. NY. 1969

SOUTH AFRICAN (BOER) WAR, 1899-1902
Caernarfonshire Record Office
Poole XM/759/D-4
List of Caernarfon Men who served in the South African War

INDEX

DROS URDDAS CYMRU